The Encyclopedia of
DOUBLE BASS DRUMMING
REVISED EDITION

By Bobby Rondinelli and Michael Lauren

Modern Drummer Publisher/CEO **David Frangioni**

Senior Art Director - **Scott Beinstock**

Director Of Content - **Mark Griffith**

Book restoration, layout, music notation - **Terry Branam**

Edited by William F. Miller

Original design and layout by Michele M. Newhouse

© Copyright 2000, 2022 Modern Drummer Media, LLC.
International Copyright Secured
All Rights Reserved
Printed in the USA

Any unauthorized duplication of this book or
its contents is a violation of copyright laws.

Published by:
Modern Drummer Media, LLC.
1279 W Palmetto Park Rd
PO Box 276064
Boca Raton, FL 33427

Subscribe to *Modern Drummer* at: www.moderndrummer.com/subscribe

**For fun and educational videos, subscribe to the
"Modern Drummer Official" YouTube channel.**

Contents

Introduction, Acknowledgments, Key		3
Getting Started With Double Bass		4
Two Bass Drums Versus A Double Pedal		5
Applying Double Bass		5

Chapter 1.	Starters	8
Chapter 2.	Two Consecutive 16th Notes	12
Chapter 3.	Three Consecutive 16th Notes	16
Chapter 4.	Four Consecutive 16th Notes	19
Chapter 5.	Five To Sixteen Consecutive 16th Notes	24
Chapter 6.	8th-Note Triplets	31
Chapter 7.	16th-Note Triplets	36
Chapter 8.	32nd-Notes and 32nd-Note Triplets	45
Chapter 9.	The Blues	49
Chapter 10.	8th Notes	52
Chapter 11.	Power Threes	54
Chapter 12.	Linear Cross Rhythms	69
Chapter 13.	Linear Cross-Rhythm Combinations	70
Chapter 14.	Fast Track Double Bass	70

New Chapters by Bobby Rondinelli 72

Chapter 15.	Starters—Double Strokes	72
Chapter 16.	Feet Only	74
Chapter 17.	Binary Beats and Fills	76
Chapter 18.	Feet Only—Triplets	84
Chapter 19.	Ternary Beats and Fills	85
Chapter 20.	Skiplets	92
Chapter 21.	Turn the Beat Around (Turnarounds)	96
Chapter 22.	The Ladder	99
Chapter 23.	Double-Stroke Hands, Single-Stroke Feet	101

Double Bass Time Line	103
Double Bass Discography	113

Introduction

The Encyclopedia Of Double Bass Drumming is a progressive approach for developing a comprehensive double bass drum or double pedal drumming style. By practicing the materials found in this book your ability to play double bass will greatly improve.

This book has been written right-foot lead for practical notational purposes.

However, there really are no rules when playing double bass. In fact, various "footing" possibilities have been included where appropriate. (The term "footings" is used throughout the book to describe the foot combinations [right or left] to be used for a given exercise.) You may find it more comfortable to lead with your left foot. Experiment and see what works best for you. Also, you can play the examples with either a heels-up or heels-down approach.

The authors believe that beginning to advanced drummers will find this encyclopedia beneficial and rewarding. All chapters that contain beats also include basic warm-ups, fills, and a combination of beats and fills in various phrase lengths. If a double bass drum rhythm presents a problem, try playing it first with your hands. Once you can hear the rhythm, your feet will learn it more quickly.

Finally, this book incorporates a variety of styles including rock, funk, and blues. Double bass drumming has no stylistic limitations.

Acknowledgments

In Memory of Michael Joos and William F. Miller. Their vision and input helped make this book possible.

Bobby Rondinelli would like to thank Ludwig drums, Paiste cymbals and gongs, Gibraltar hardware, Czarcie Kopyto pedals, Vater drumsticks, Aquarian drumheads, Gon Bops cowbells and percussion, Ultimate Ear in-ear monitors, Miktek microphones, Snareweight, Canopus accessories, Hansenfutz, Prologix practice pads and Cympad.

Michael Lauren would like to thank Yamaha Drums, Zildjian Cymbals and Sticks, Remo Drum Heads, SkyGel Damper Pads, Protection Racket Drum Cases, Road Crew.

Key

Hi-Hat   Tom   Snare   BD I   BD II

A NOTE FROM THE PUBLISHER

The day I discovered double bass drum playing changed my drumming forever. Now I had another set of hands but they're actually my feet?! Plus, I could augment fills, grooves, and endless other ideas by combining hands and feet. Double Bass Drumming is truly limitless.

Bobby Rondinelli is a pioneer and innovator on both playing and teaching Double Bass Drumming.

You now have in your possession a treasure trove of exercises that when practiced and utilized in your playing will elevate your double bass drumming very quickly and effectively.

Bobby uses this book for his own playing and we at *Modern Drummer* are privileged to be publisher to his work and the advancement of your playing!

Thank you Bobby and thank YOU, the reader, for taking your playing to the next level with Bobby Rondinelli's *Encyclopedia of Double Bass Drumming*.

David Frangioni
CEO/Publisher of Modern Drummer Publications, Inc.

Getting Started With Double Bass

Although there are no rules or absolutes when playing double bass, here are a few suggestions and concepts to think about when first getting started.

Where you sit in relation to your bass drum (or drums) and how high or low you sit are probably the first things you should consider. Everybody sits differently, but your seat should be positioned where, when your arms are relaxed at your side and your elbows are bent at about a 90° angle, your sticks can reach the center of the snare drum. When your hands are at their lowest point, they should not interfere with the up and down motion of your legs.

How close you position yourself to the drum is also an important factor. If you sit too far back, you're probably going to experience back problems. But if you're too close, your legs will eventually cramp up. Your legs should always be in a natural position. Finding the proper sitting balance for your body type is critical for relaxed playing.

In general, you should sit at a height where your thighs are parallel to the floor. Of course, experiment with different seat heights until you feel comfortable. Don't forget to check how your left foot feels on the hi-hat as well as the second bass drum. Your feet should be in a natural position in relation to the pedal board.

The position of your feet on the pedals is the next thing to consider. Finding the "sweet spot" to get the most volume, speed, and control with the least amount of expended energy is your goal. Here's one way to find that spot: Place your foot at the top of the pedal board. Play simple quarter notes. Then slide your foot down in one-inch increments until you reach the point where your volume doubles with no change in effort. *That's* your "sweet spot." (When you go past that point you'll find it more difficult to play.) You might want to put a piece of tape on your pedal board to mark the sweet spot. Follow the same procedure for the other pedal.

Adjusting the pedal beater position is another point to consider. The shaft should be set at a height where the beater strikes as close to the center of the head as possible. If you're looking for more power, the beater's starting point should be as far back as possible, without hitting your foot. Remember, there are no absolutes.

Pedal tension is also very personal. A good place to begin to find the feel that's right for you is a medium tension. But keep in mind that if the tension is too loose, the beater will flop dead on the head. And a very tight spring will have you fighting the pedal. You should be able to push on the pedal with a strong but relaxed motion and get a comfortable response.

While you can play double bass with a heels-up or heels-down approach, we recommend that you play the pedals with the balls of your feet, keeping your heels close to the pedal boards but not planted on them. (Don't lift your heels too high, as that will create a lot of strain in your legs.) Your foot should remain low to the ground. Be sure to keep your legs as relaxed as possible.

What about head tension? Is it better to play with a bass drum head that is dead (loose) or live (tight)? Again, you'll have to experiment. Some successful double bass players prefer a tight tension, others swear by a loose one. A big consideration is the effects tension changes have on your bass drum *sound*. Start with a medium tension (with slight finger pressure the head should easily push in) and go from there.

Two Bass Drums Versus A Double Pedal

What are the differences between using two bass drums and using a double pedal? Both setups have their own advantages and disadvantages. Double pedals give you a more even articulation, attack, and sound. Two bass drums give you a wider, broader sound. Using two bass drums of the same size, but tuned differently, or playing two different-size bass drums, can give you a variety of pitches to work with.

Of course, the convenience and portability of playing a double pedal are obvious. (And most studio and live-sound engineers prefer only dealing with one bass drum!) Two bass drums also bring about the challenge of increased physical movement, because they expand the kit. With double bass you might have to stretch a little to reach your toms and cymbals.

To a certain extent, singles are easier to play on double pedals, just like singles played by the hands are easier on one drum than split between two. But broken-up figures are a bit easier to play on two bass drums.

Applying Double Bass

When is the best time to play double bass? As in all musical situations, good taste should always prevail. Remember, too much of a good thing can quickly turn into a very bad thing. Pick your spots for the greatest musical effect. You can play busy with taste, but music without *contrast* becomes boring.

Double bass works great at the end of phrases and sections of tunes. The power of double bass can take the music to a higher dynamic level. But be careful not to "overplay the music." Use double bass in spurts. Look for the holes in the music to maximize its effect.

Double bass should enhance an already "complete" drummer. Double bass should not be a substitute for a weak single foot. And don't forget the hi-hat pedal: It shouldn't be a footrest when you're not playing double bass. Musical hi-hat work is a very important quality of a complete drummer.

Double bass techniques are great when integrated into grooves or when used as an embellishment of a rhythmic figure, just as you would use ruffs and flams to embellish a figure played with your hands. Fills are a terrific place to use double bass, too. Of course, double bass is *great* for soloing. You can lay down an ostinato with it, integrate it into combination hand/foot rhythmic figures, or build huge climaxes with it.

Use your double bass technique for musical innovation and to propel the music forward. And one other important piece of advice: Don't play double bass drums just because they are there. Play them only when their inclusion adds something *meaningful* to the music.

Chapter 1 Starters

- Starters are to get your feet going without worrying about your hands.
- These preliminary exercises isolate and help develop your weak foot.
- You're only as strong as your weakest limb.
- These exercises should be played at controlled tempos for long periods of time in order to develop stamina. .
- Practice at a variety of dynamic levels and tempos.
- Don't neglect the accents.
- Exercises 8–12 are single stroke rolls played between the feet. Single-stroke rolls are the foundation of double bass drumming.
- Play each exercise for at least one minute without stopping.
- Accuracy and evenness should never be sacrificed for speed.
- These exercises can be played on and off the kit.
- Tapping your feet on the floor *is* practicing and *is* beneficial.
- Work with a metronome or drum machine.

Beats

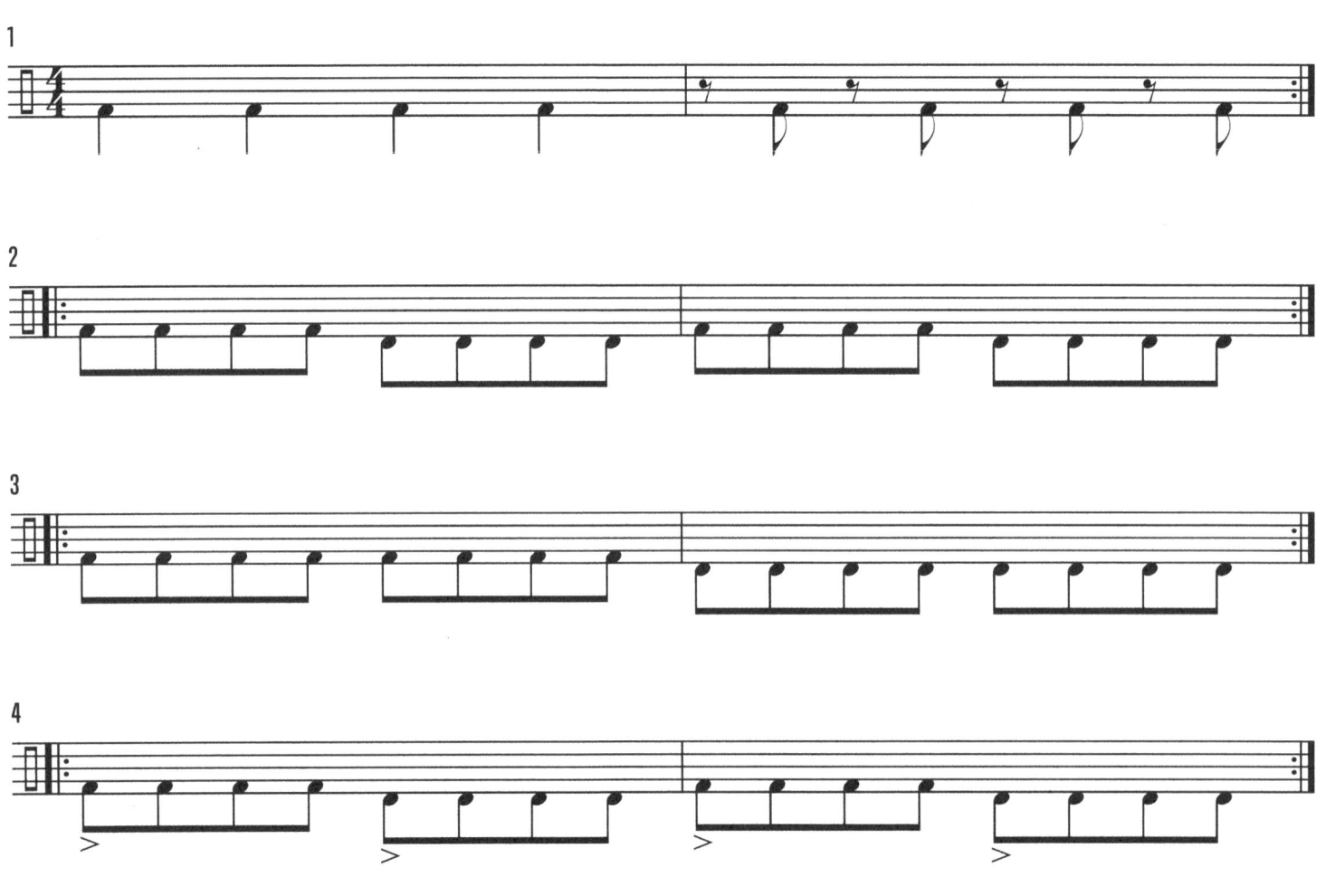

Chapter 2 Two Consecutive 16th Notes

- This chapter includes warm-ups, beats, and fills containing two consecutive 16th notes.

- Although these two-note ideas can be played with one foot, the ability to play two notes evenly and powerfully between your feet must be developed.

- The warm-up exercises help develop your coordination by focusing solely on repeated two-note patterns.

- Make your feet sound consistent on their own.

- Beats 13–18 are more difficult. Feel free to come back to them at a later date.

- Beats 16–18 have syncopated snare drum rhythms.

- Beats 19 and 20 are two-bar phrases. Combine any of the previous beats to create your own two-, four-, and eight-bar phrases.

- Fills 21–30 are one-measure fills. Combine them with the previous beats.

- The fills are written with snare drum and bass drums only. Try other orchestrations. For example:
  1. Right hand on snare drum and left hand on high tom.
  2. Right hand on floor tom and left hand on high tom.

- Fill 31 is an example of a two-bar phrase containing a short fill.

- Fills 32 and 33 are examples of phrases that include a one-bar fill.

- Fill 34 illustrates a fill longer than one measure.

- Be creative with the length of your fills. They don't have to start and end on beat 1 of a measure.

Warm-Ups

1

2

3
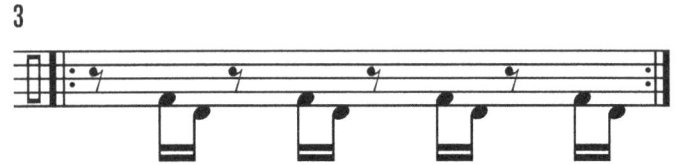

4

Beats

19

20

Fills

21

22

23

24

25

26

27

28

29

30

31

32

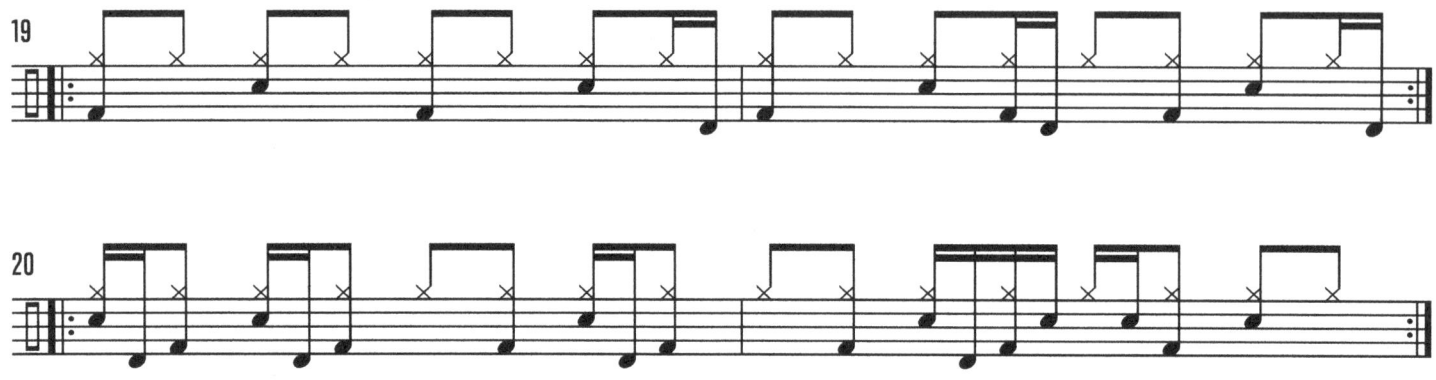

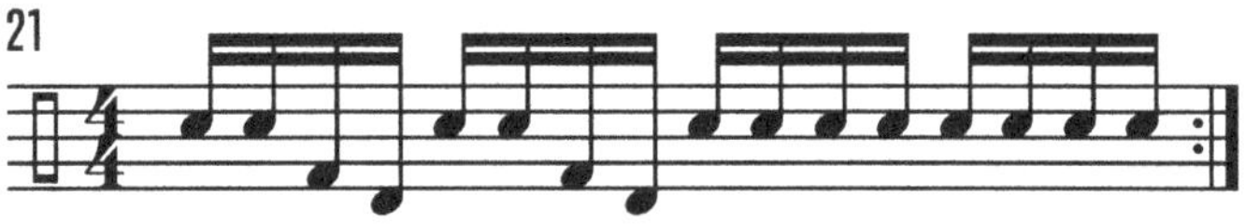

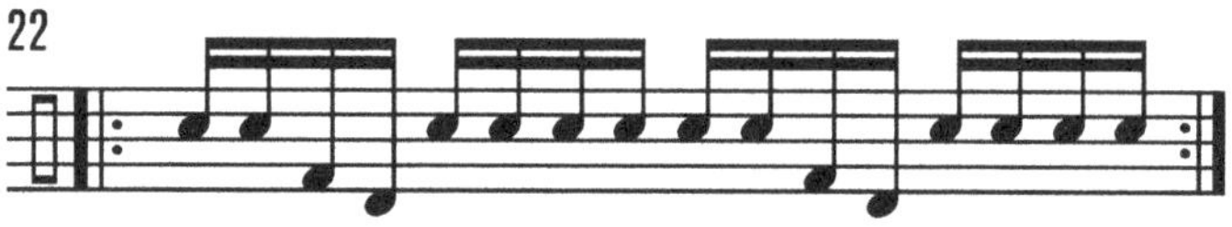

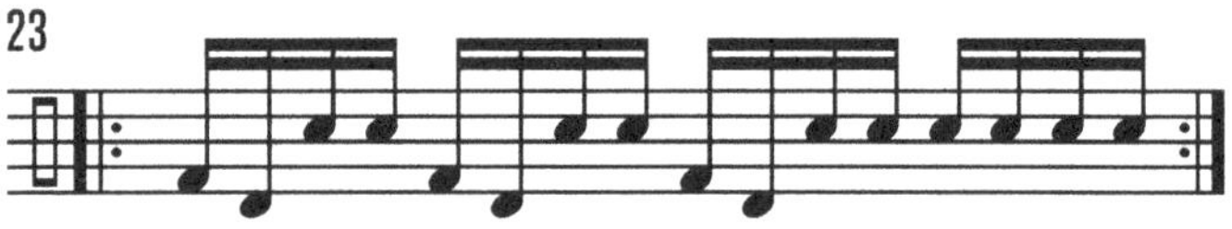

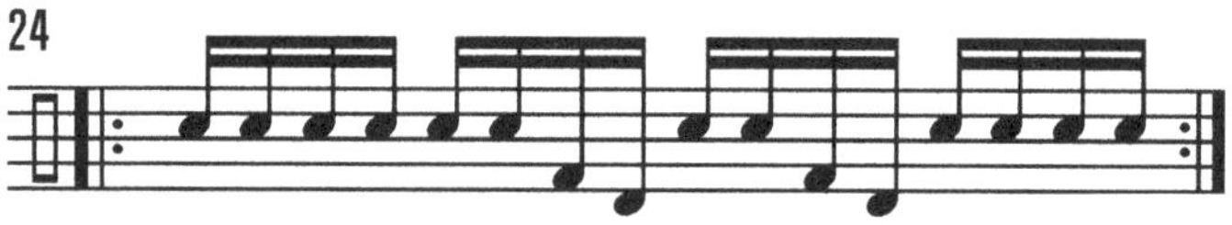

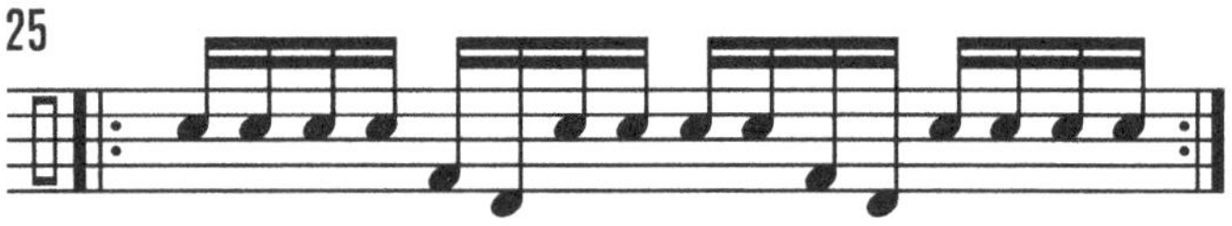

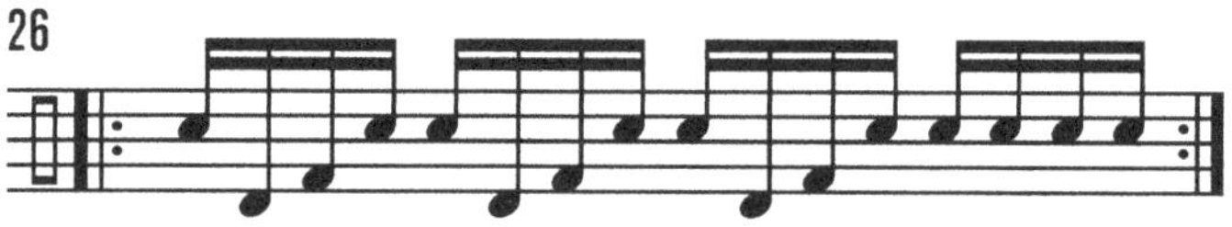

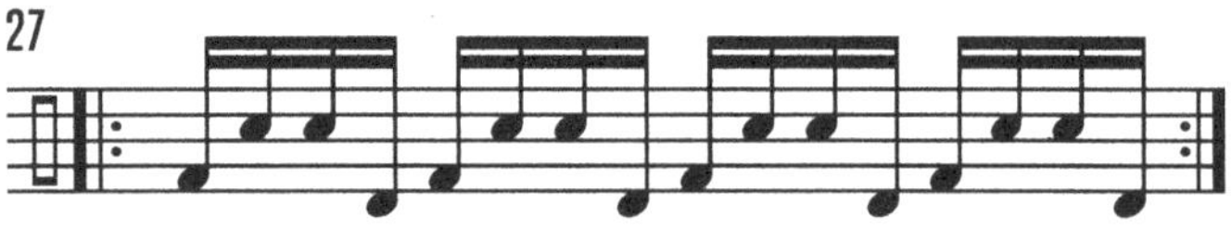

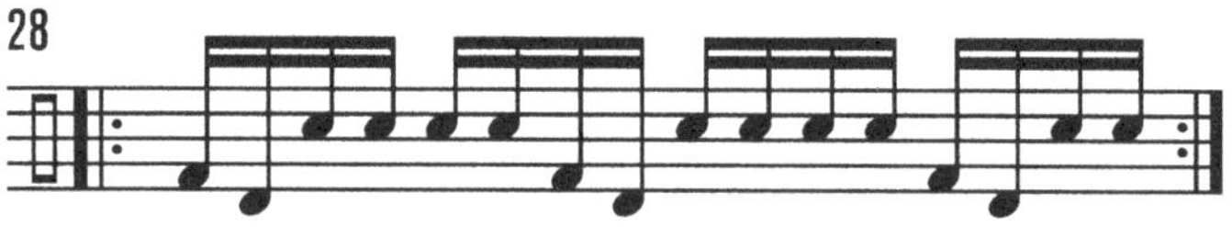

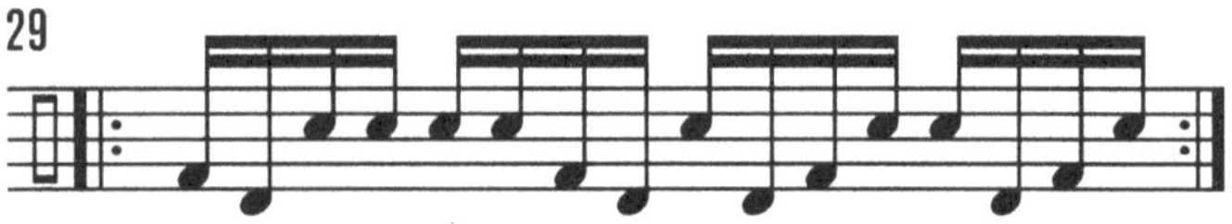

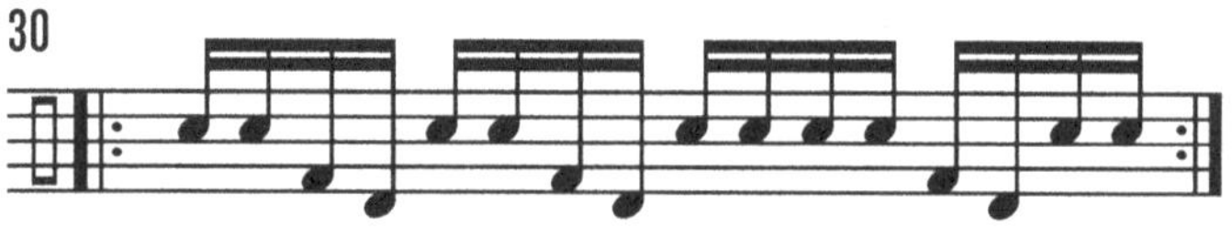

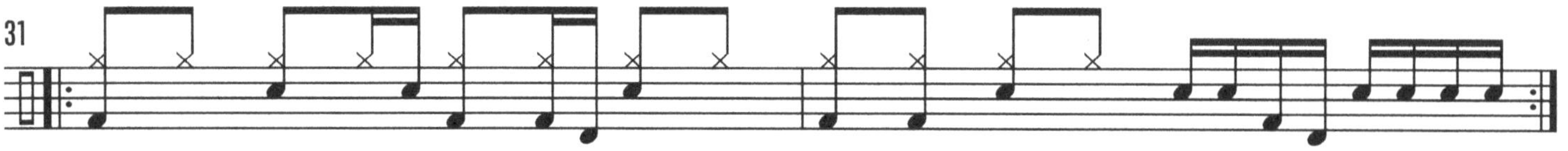

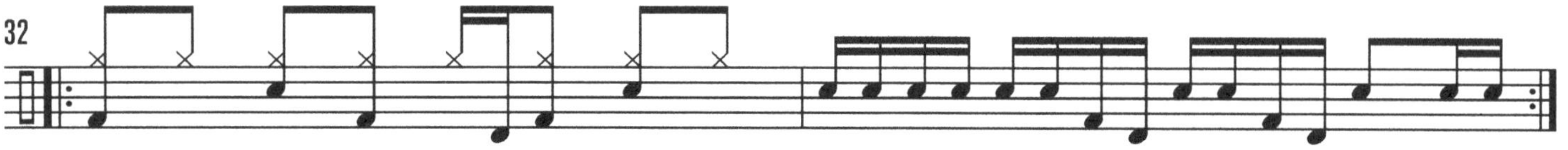

Chapter 3: Three Consecutive 16th Notes

- The most common way to play consecutive three-note patterns is either RLR or LRL.
- The additional footings of the warm-ups will make you aware of other possibilities, while further developing your coordination, balance, and control.
- Fills 29–32 are four-bar phrases illustrating different fill lengths.

Warm-Ups

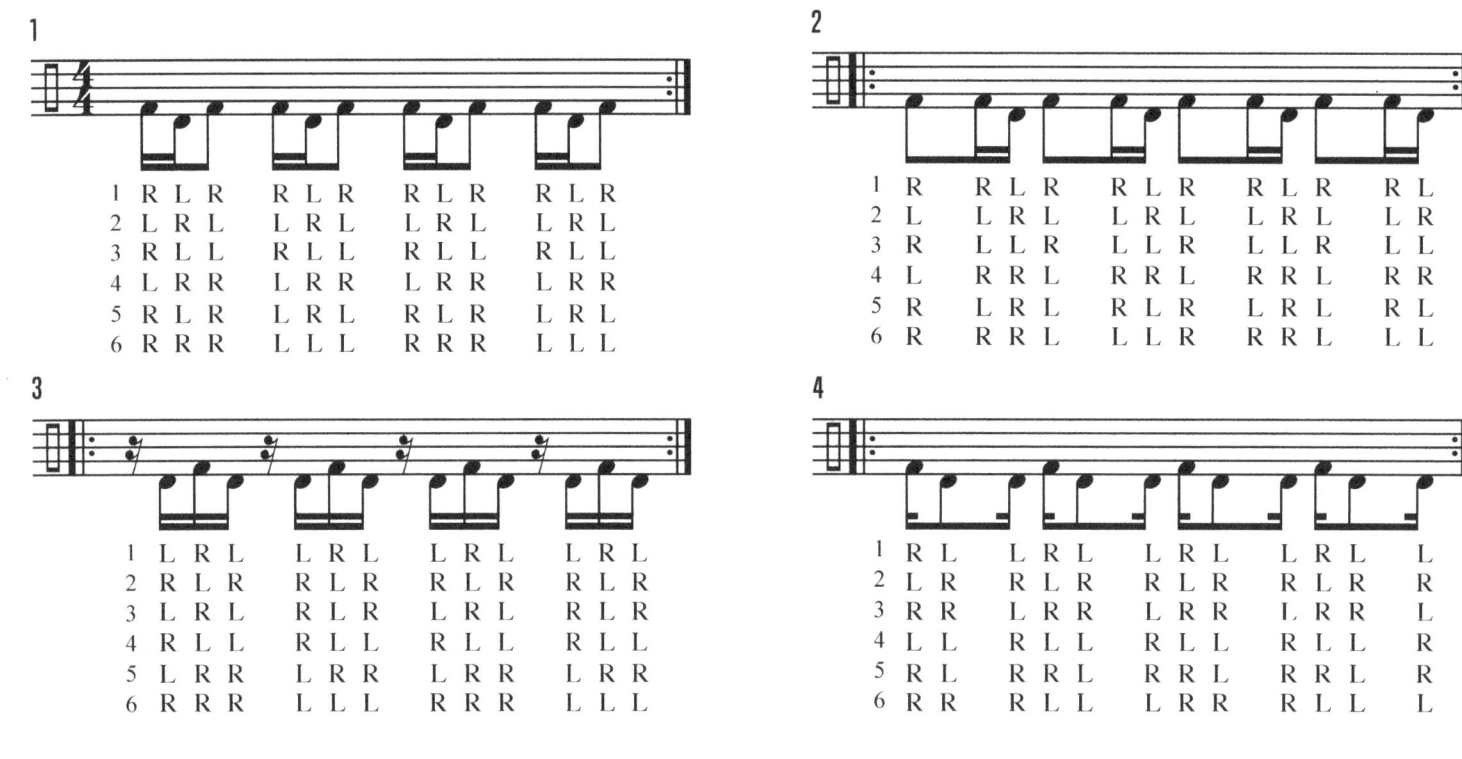

Beats

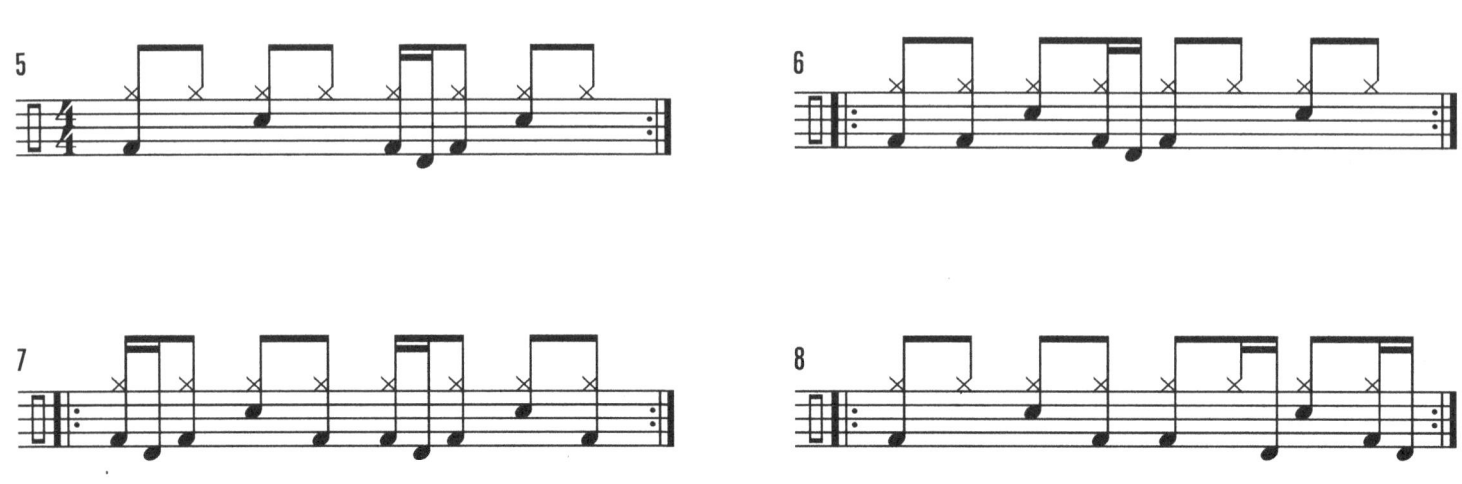

Encyclopedia Of Double Bass Drumming

Fills

Chapter 4: Four Consecutive 16th Notes

- "Fours" are difficult when leading with your weak foot. We suggest that you don't avoid this problem. Working on the difficult things makes you a stronger drummer.
- All of the patterns can be played leading with either your strong or weak foot. However, in the real world, what you play and how it sounds is more important than how you play it.
- Practicing is about working on what you can't do well.
- Pay attention when the snare and bass drum hit together. Make sure they're in unison. Don't flam them.
- Double bass can get funky. Check out Beats 17 and 18.
- Fill 31 incorporates two-, three-, and four-consecutive-note patterns.
- Try the additional footings in each warm-up exercise.

Warm-Ups

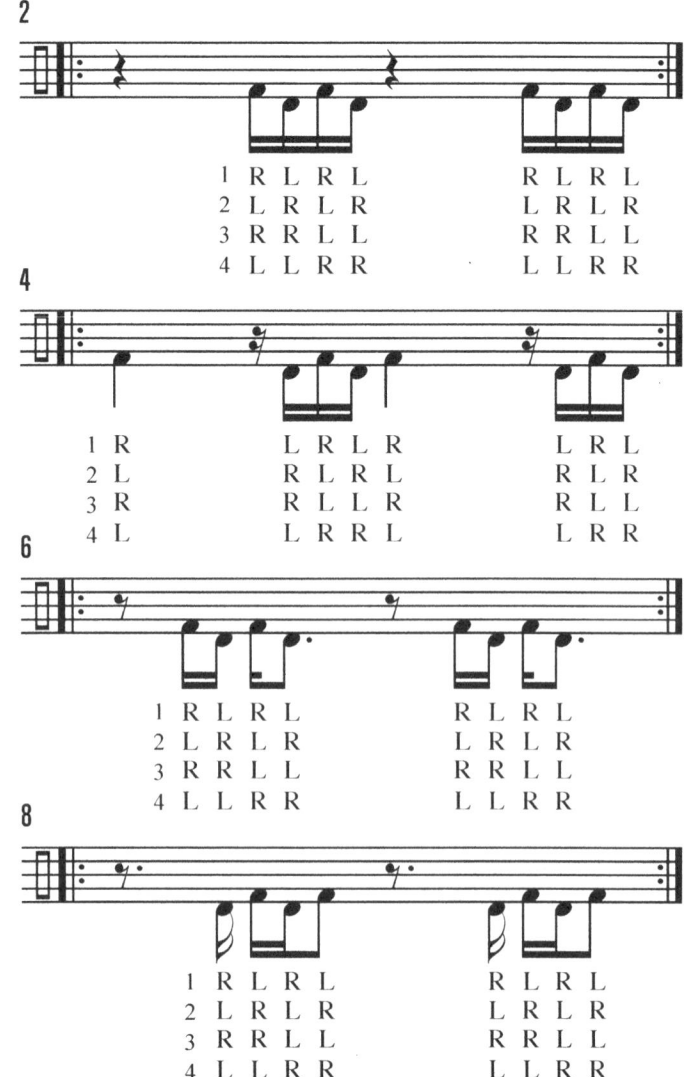

16 | Encyclopedia Of Double Bass Drumming

Beats

Fills

Chapter 5 Five To Sixteen Consecutive 16th Notes

- This section builds upon previous smaller note groupings.
- We didn't try to include every possible combination, but there are more than enough ideas here to get you started in the right direction.
- We have included more syncopated snare rhythms than in previous chapters.
- The various hand/foot exercises will open you up to the limitless possibilities of syncopated double bass drumming.
- Develop your own voice. Experiment.
- Double bass drumming is not the exclusive domain of rock, Many of the bass drum patterns here are very funky.
- Fills 39–46 demonstrate various hand patterns over continuous 16th-note double bass.

Warm-Ups

1

2

3

4

5

6

Encyclopedia Of Double Bass Drumming | 19

7

8

9

10

Beats

11

12

13

14

15

16

17

18

19

20

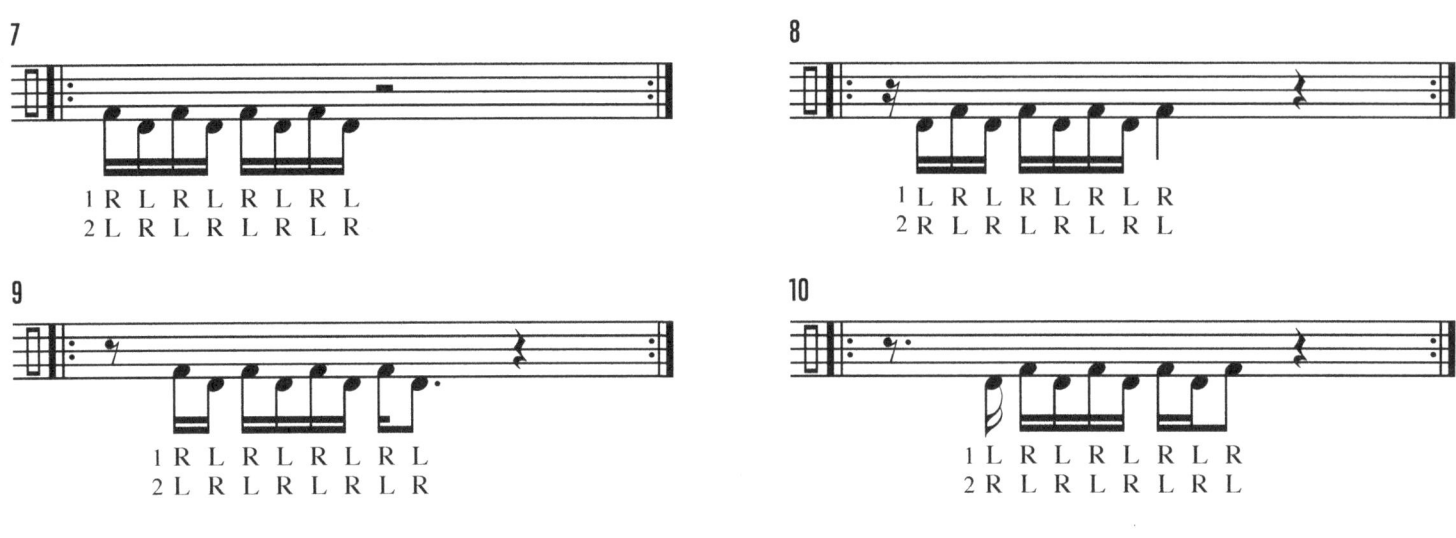

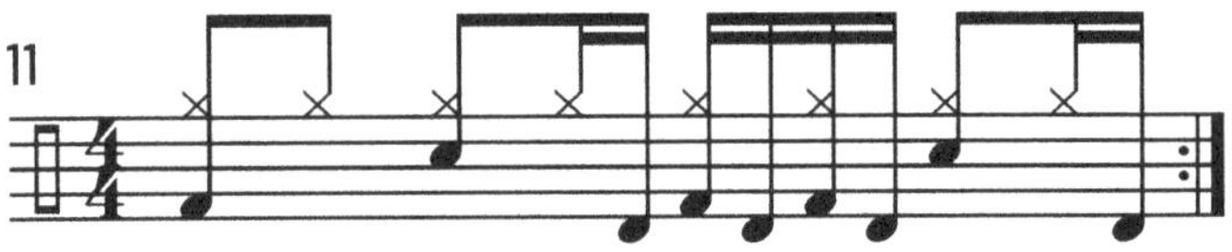

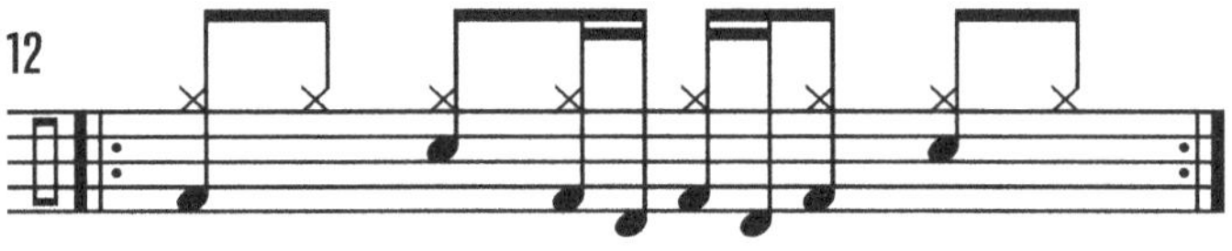

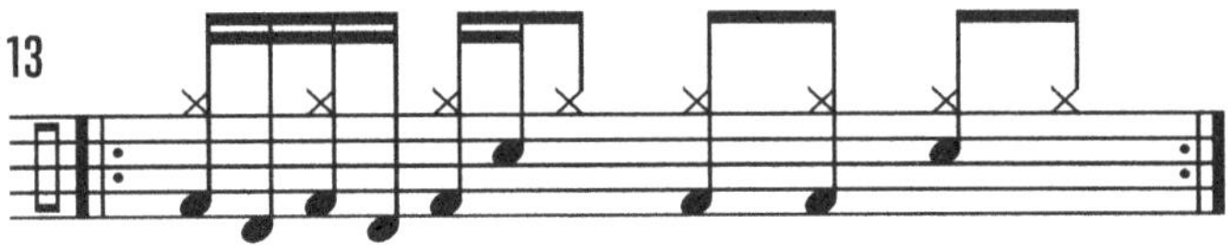

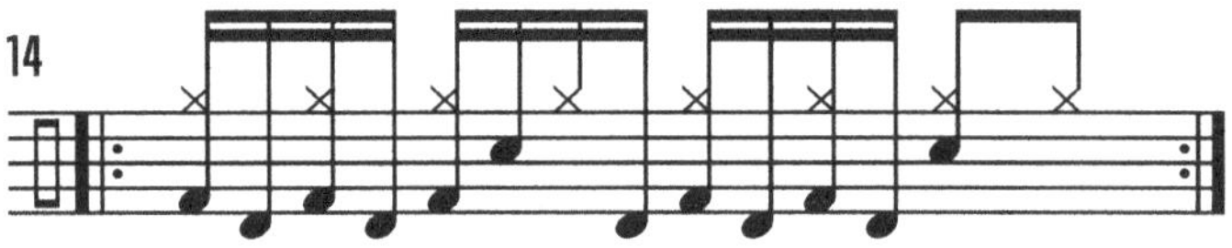

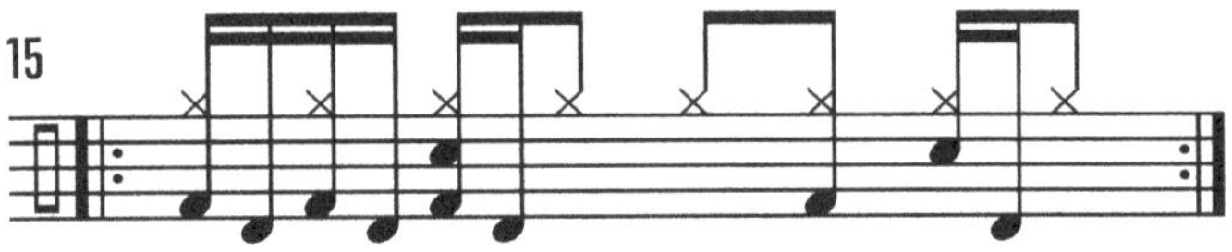

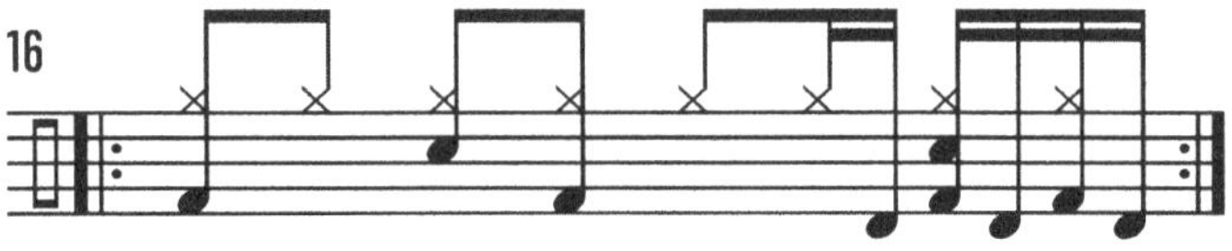

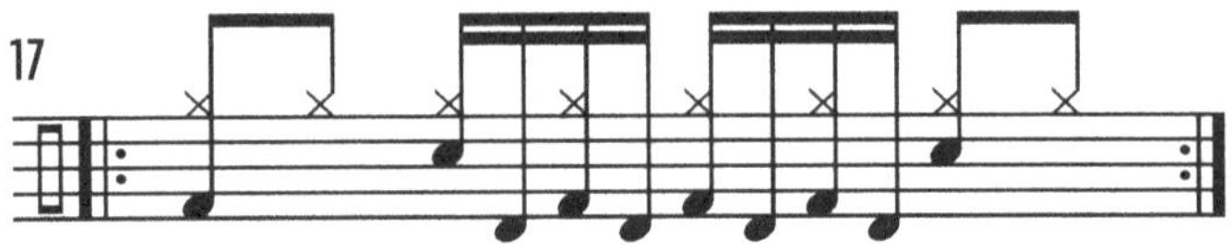

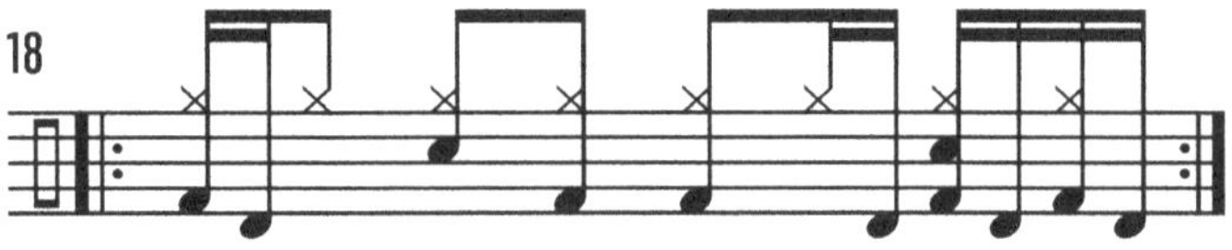

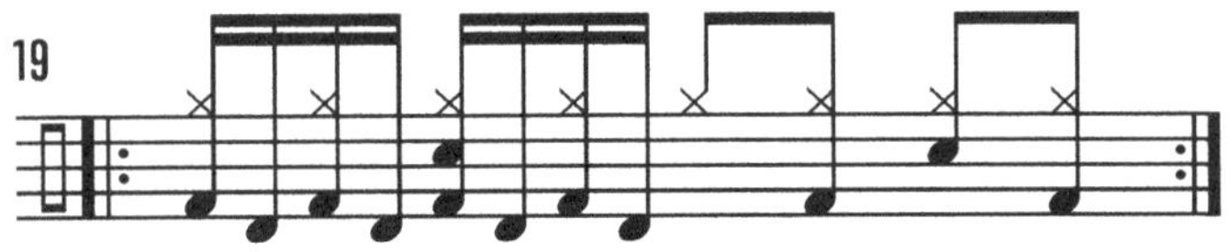

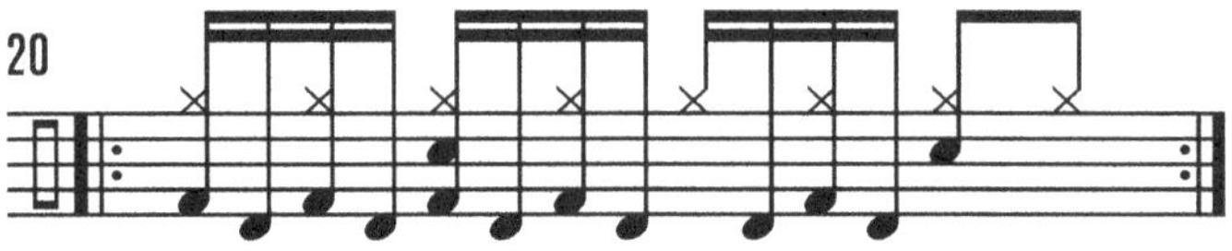

Fills

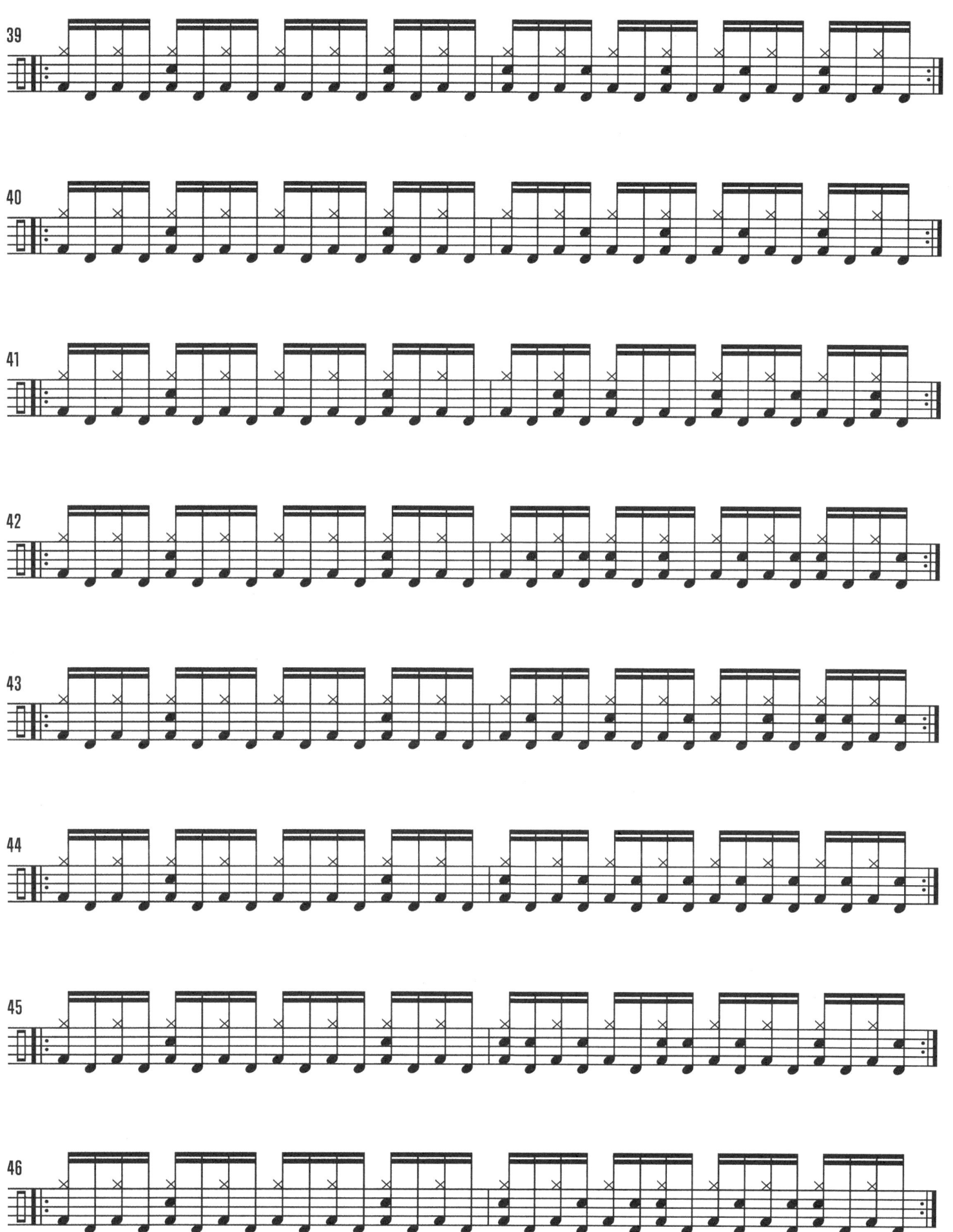

Chapter 6: 8th-Note Triplets

- The most common way to play triplets is to alternate them (RLR LRL).
- The warm-ups include a number of other footings that will help your coordination.
- Keep the triplets sounding wide and even. Don't rush them.
- Notice that when leading with your right foot the backbeat falls with your left foot.
- Some Beats in this section have more involved snare drum parts.
- Continuous shuffles are written strong-foot lead for practical purposes. (See examples 30, 31, 32, 34, 38, 39, and 71.)
- Triplets are not just used in shuffles.
- Although 8th-note triplet double bass is generally played at fast tempos, don't overlook practicing all of the exercises at slow tempos. Slow tempos are just as challenging as fast ones.
- Working in this chapter will give you a real grasp on double bass triplet technique.

Warm-Ups

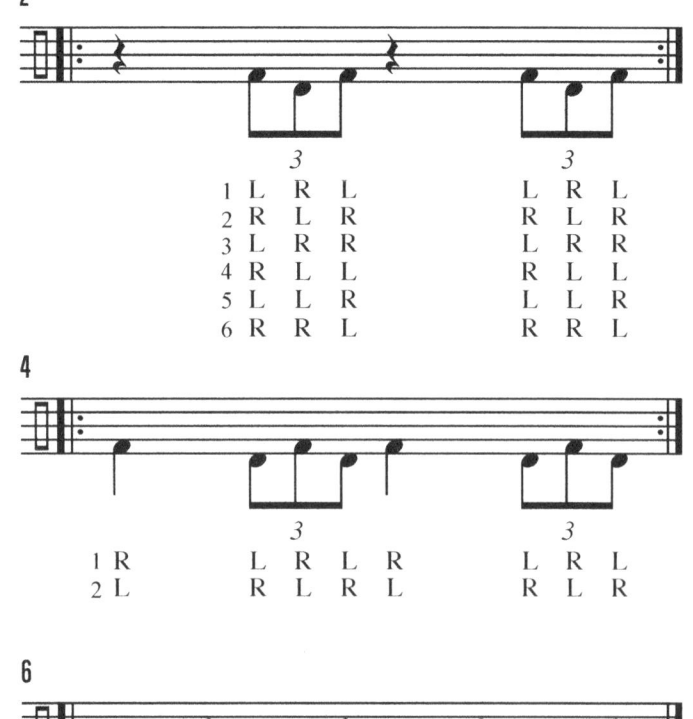

Encyclopedia Of Double Bass Drumming

7

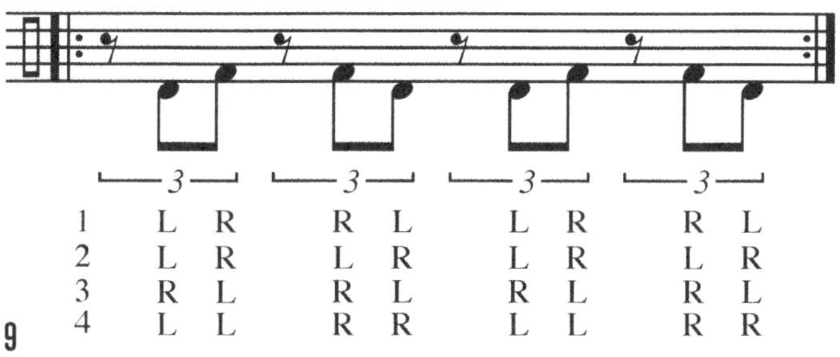

8

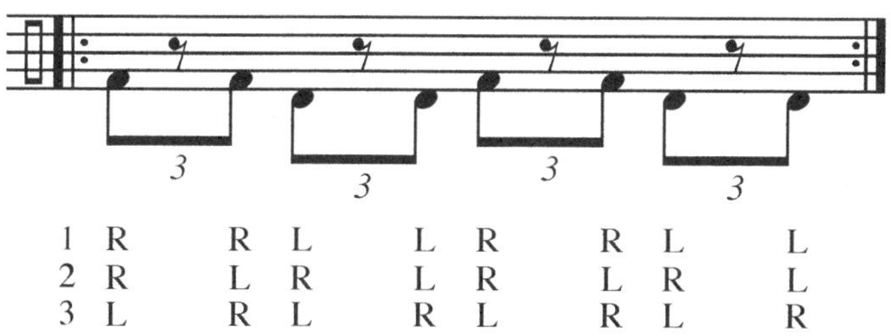

9

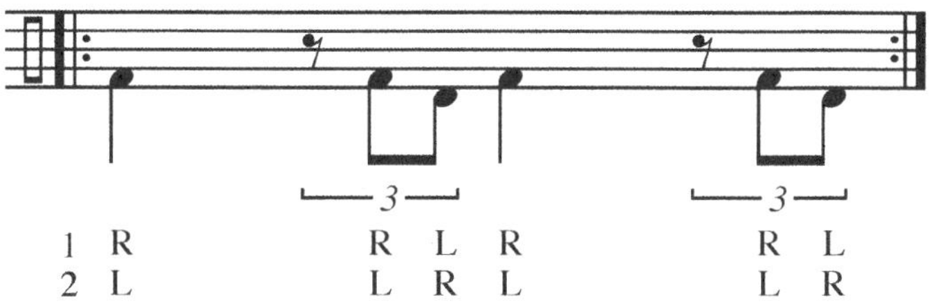

10

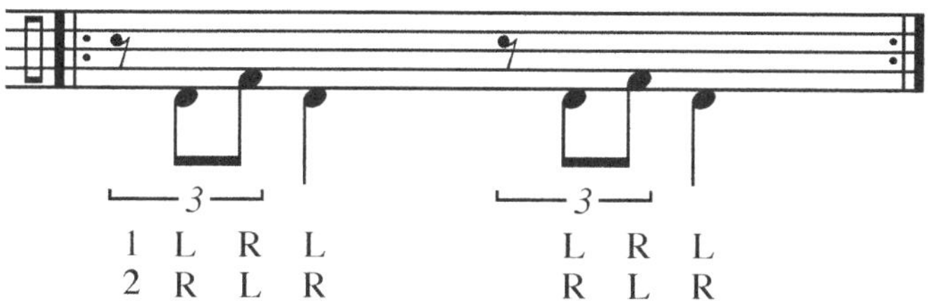

11

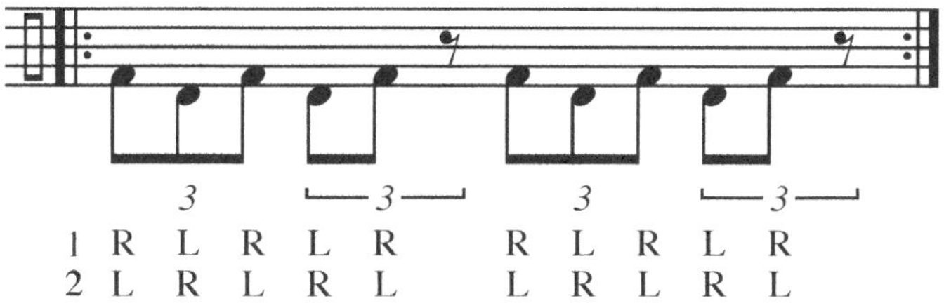

12

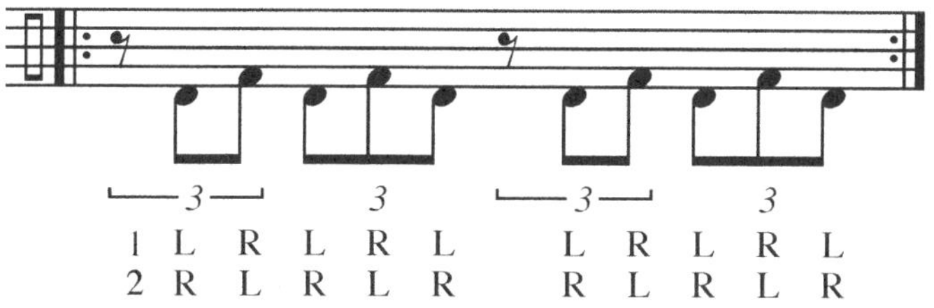

Beats

• Remember: All beats and fills are right foot lead. Other possible footings are included where written.

13

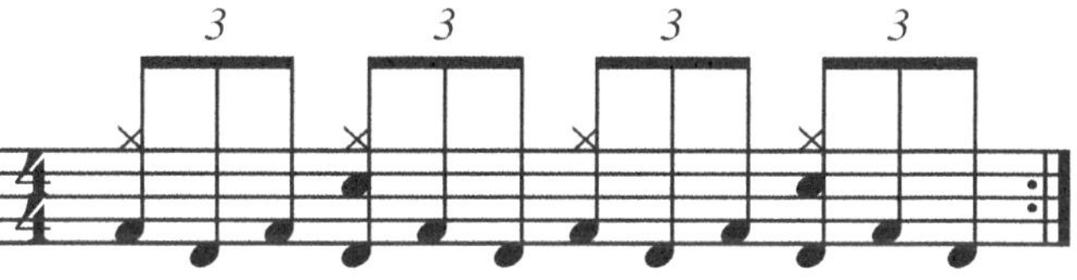

14

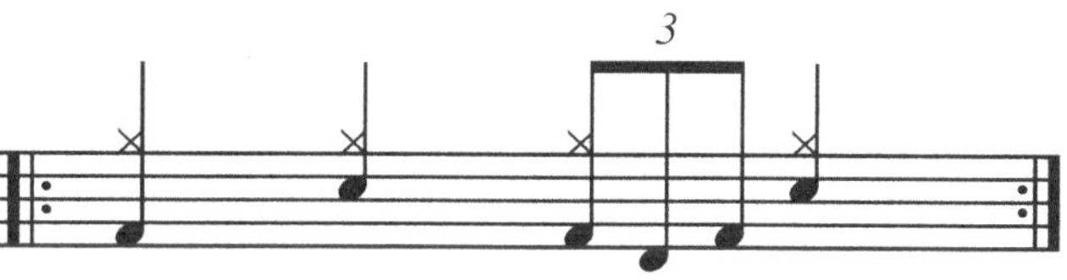

15

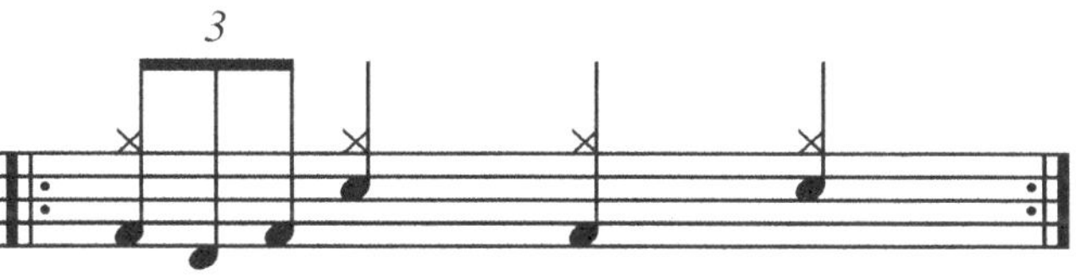

16

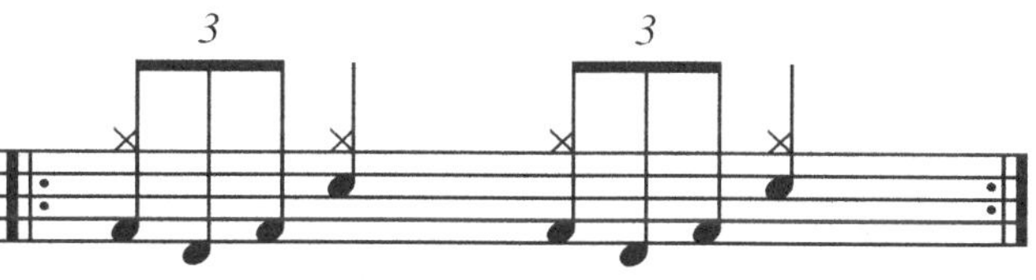

17

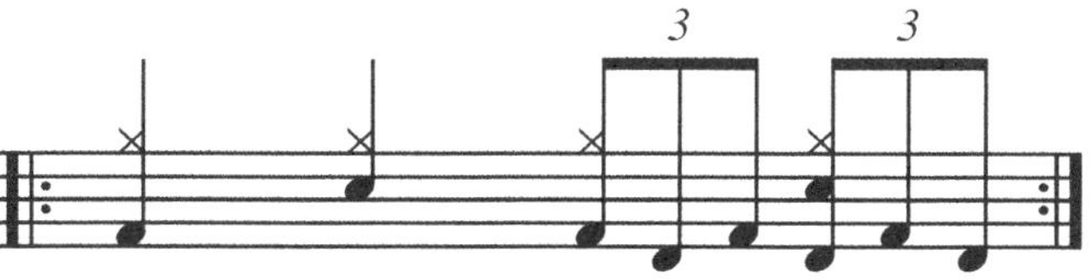

18

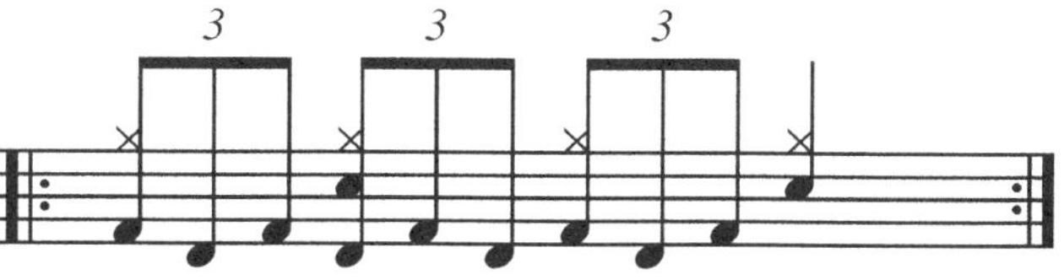

19

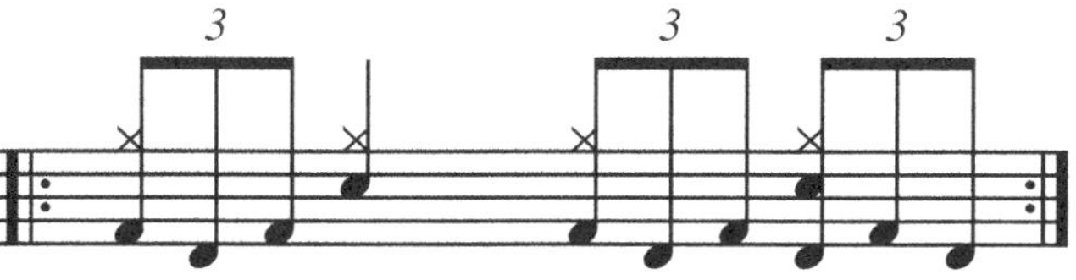

20

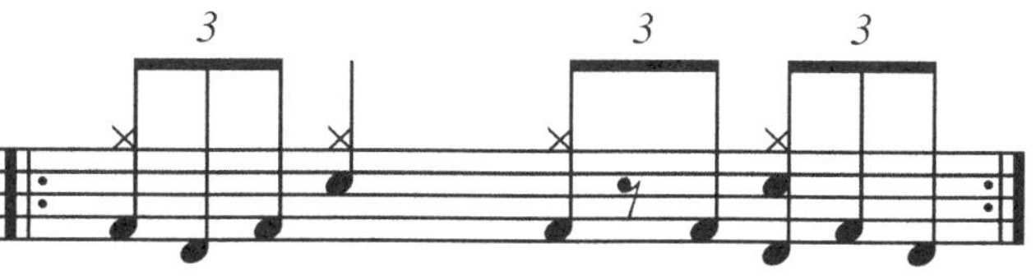

21

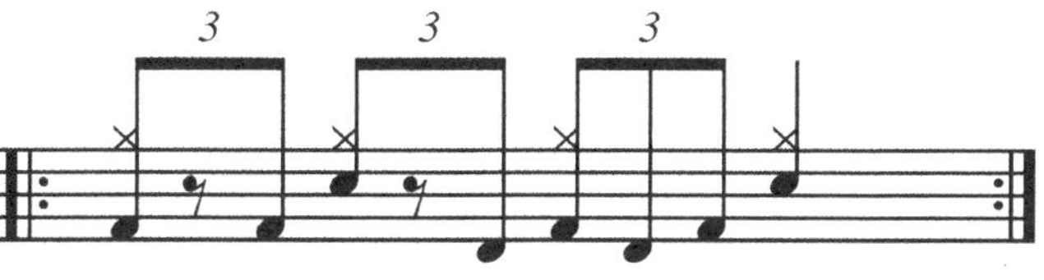

22

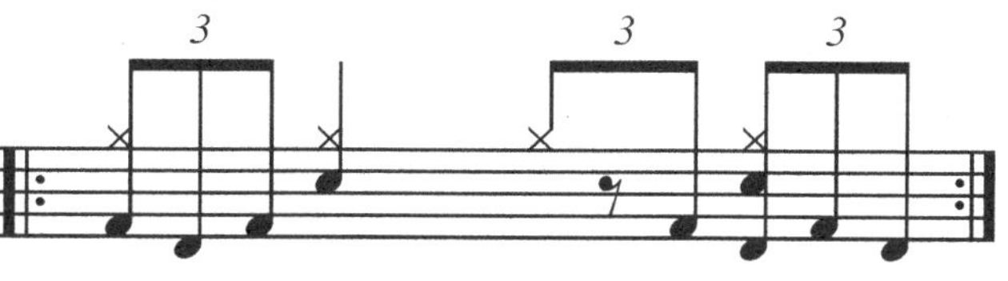

Fills

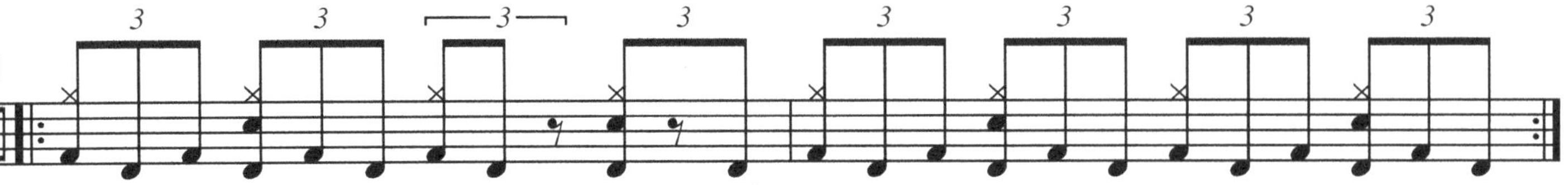

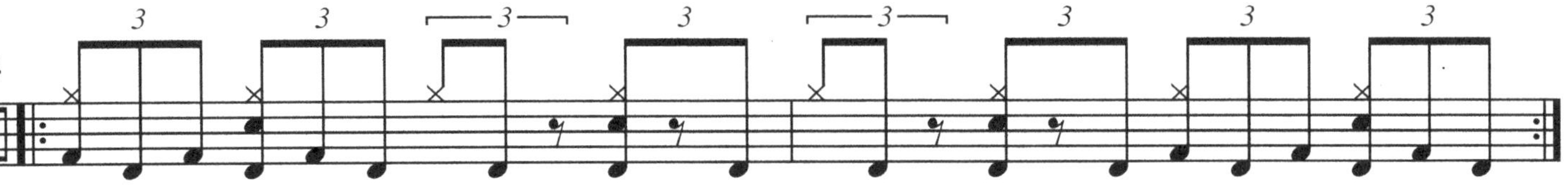

28 | Encyclopedia Of Double Bass Drumming

Chapter 7: 16th-Note Triplets

- When playing alternating 16th note triplets (right-foot lead), it's important to realize that your backbeat lands with your right foot. This is the opposite of 8th-note triplets (right-foot lead), where your backbeat lands with your left foot.

- Don't flam the snare and bass drum.

- Stay relaxed as you increase the tempo.

- Be aware of your body posture.

- Don't fight gravity. Make it work for you.

- You can swing the non-triplet 16th notes or play them straight.

- A few of the Beats and Fills that follow are not written in strong-foot notation (consistently leading with right foot). While it's good to practice patterns with all footing combinations as presented in the Warm-Ups), the ones shown are the most practical or are a good starting point.

Warm-Ups

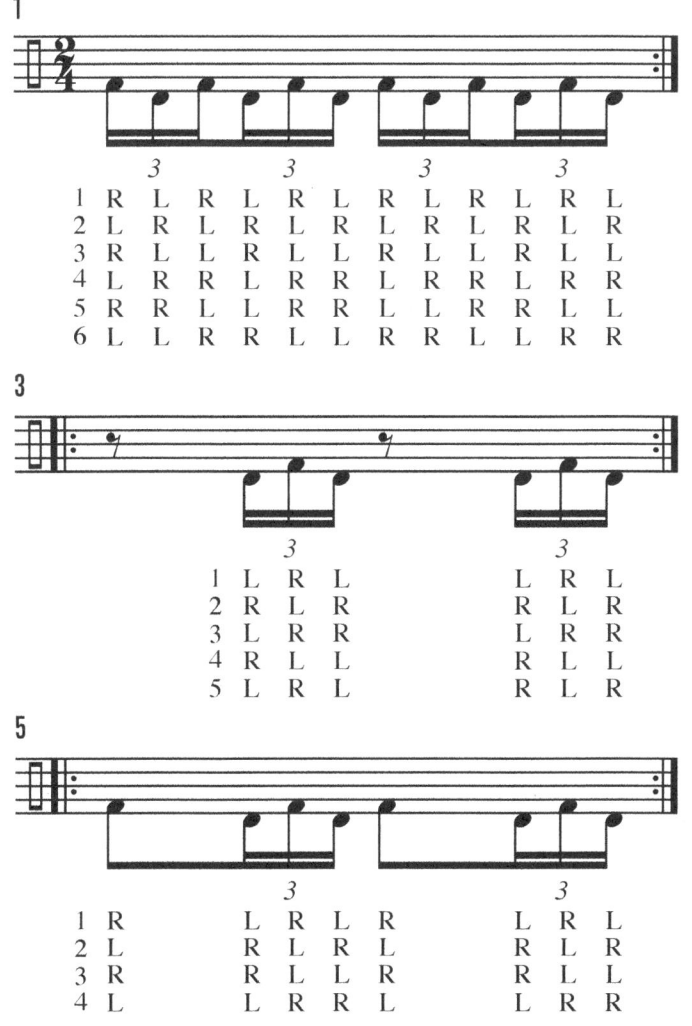

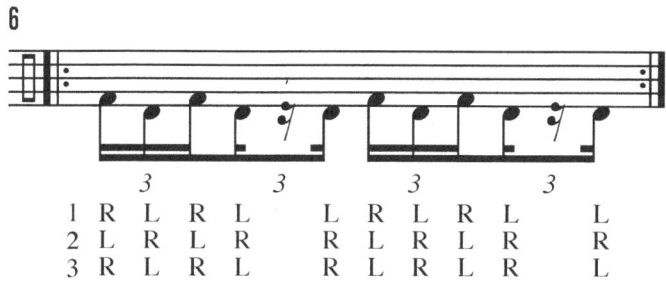

Encyclopedia Of Double Bass Drumming | 31

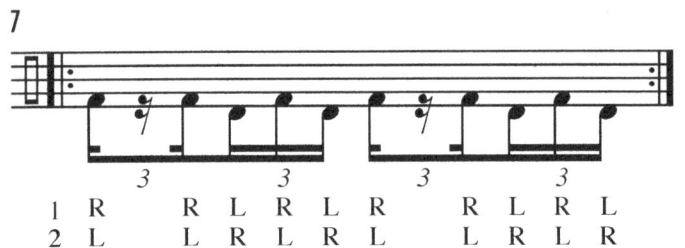

Beats

Other possible footings are written under beats and fills

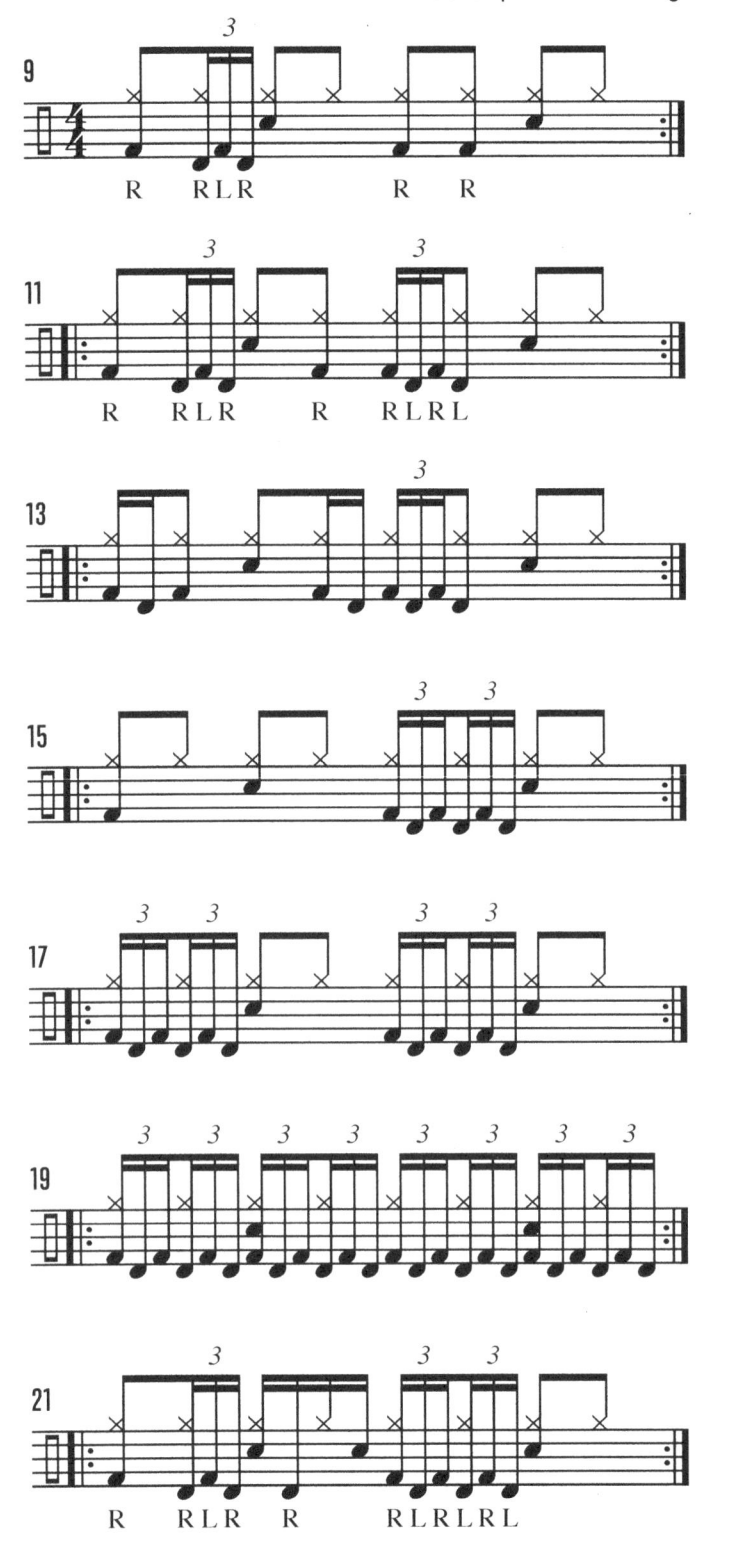
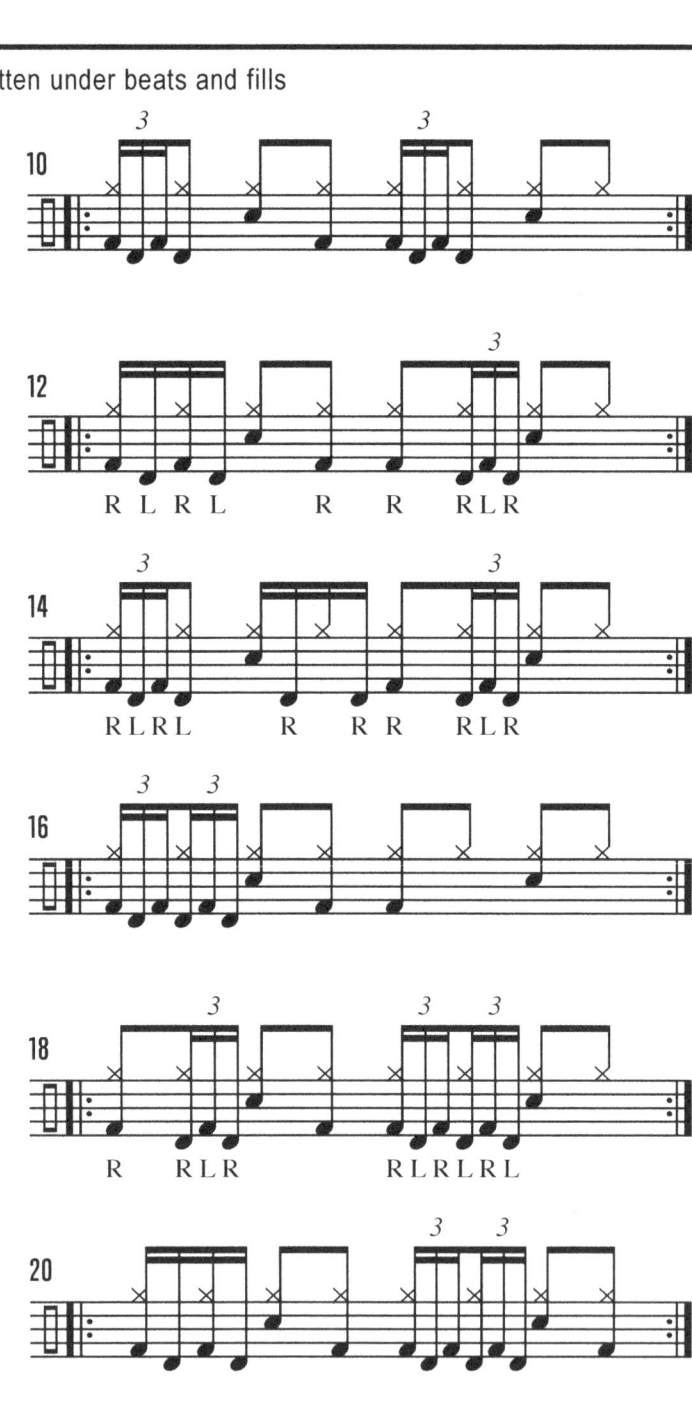

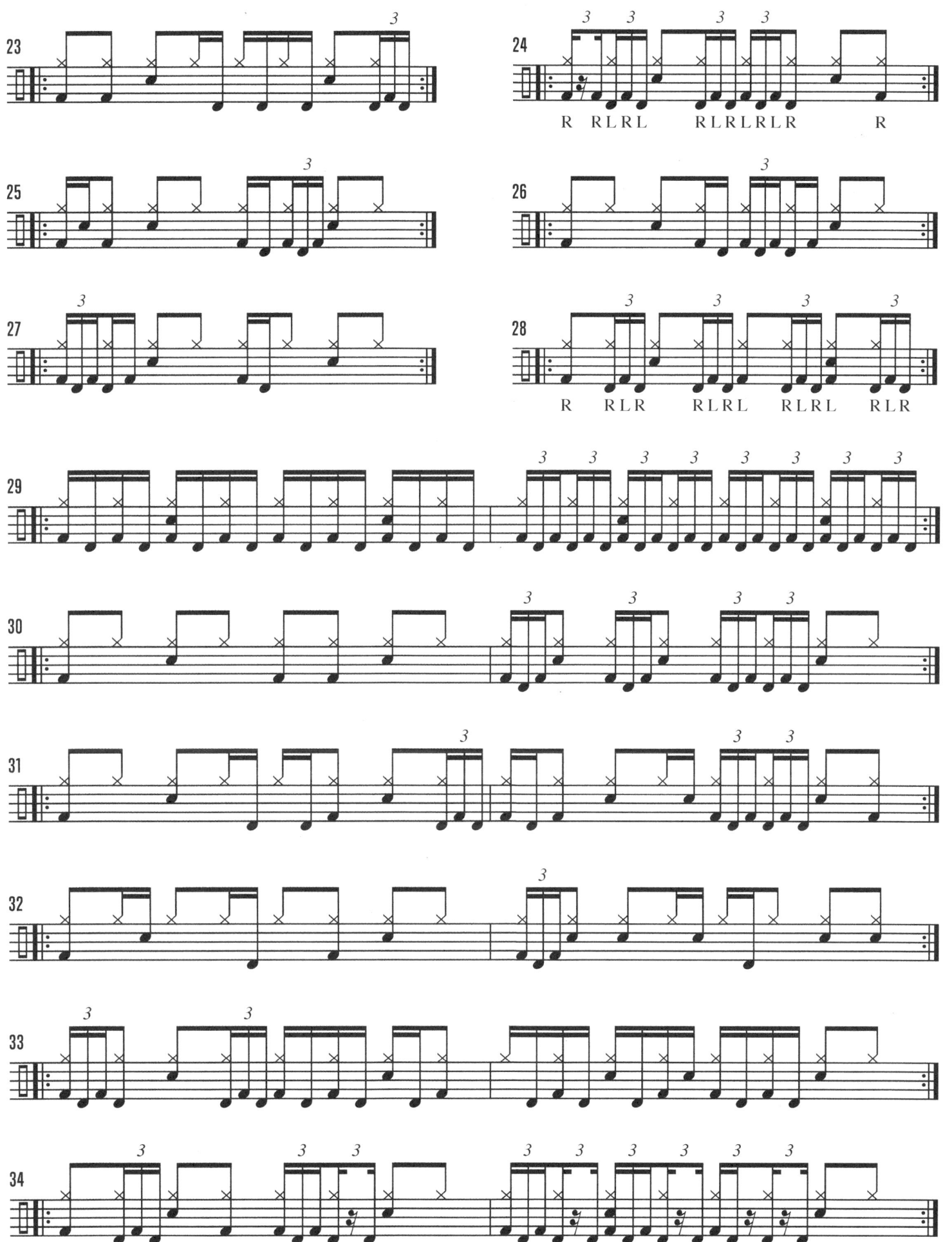

Chapter 8: 32nd Notes And 32nd-Note Triplets

- Although many of the two-stroke 32nd-note exercises can be played with one foot, two feet can be faster and more powerful than one.

- Counting is critical in this section. Count the 16th-note subdivision. Start slowly and count out loud to ensure rhythmic accuracy.

- Most of the warm-ups in this chapter combine your hands and feet.

- The warm-ups also make great fills.

- Many of the beats are very challenging, but they are not impossible.

- All of the beats are playable and can be used at a variety of tempos.

- Although all of the exercises are notated strong-foot lead, triplet patterns can turn your feet around. That's why it's important to practice strong- *and* weak-foot lead. The more versatile you are, the better drummer you'll be.

- The fills can be orchestrated between different drums. Split the hand 32nd-notes between two different drums. Try your right hand on snare and left hand on high tom.

Warm-Ups

36 | Encyclopedia Of Double Bass Drumming

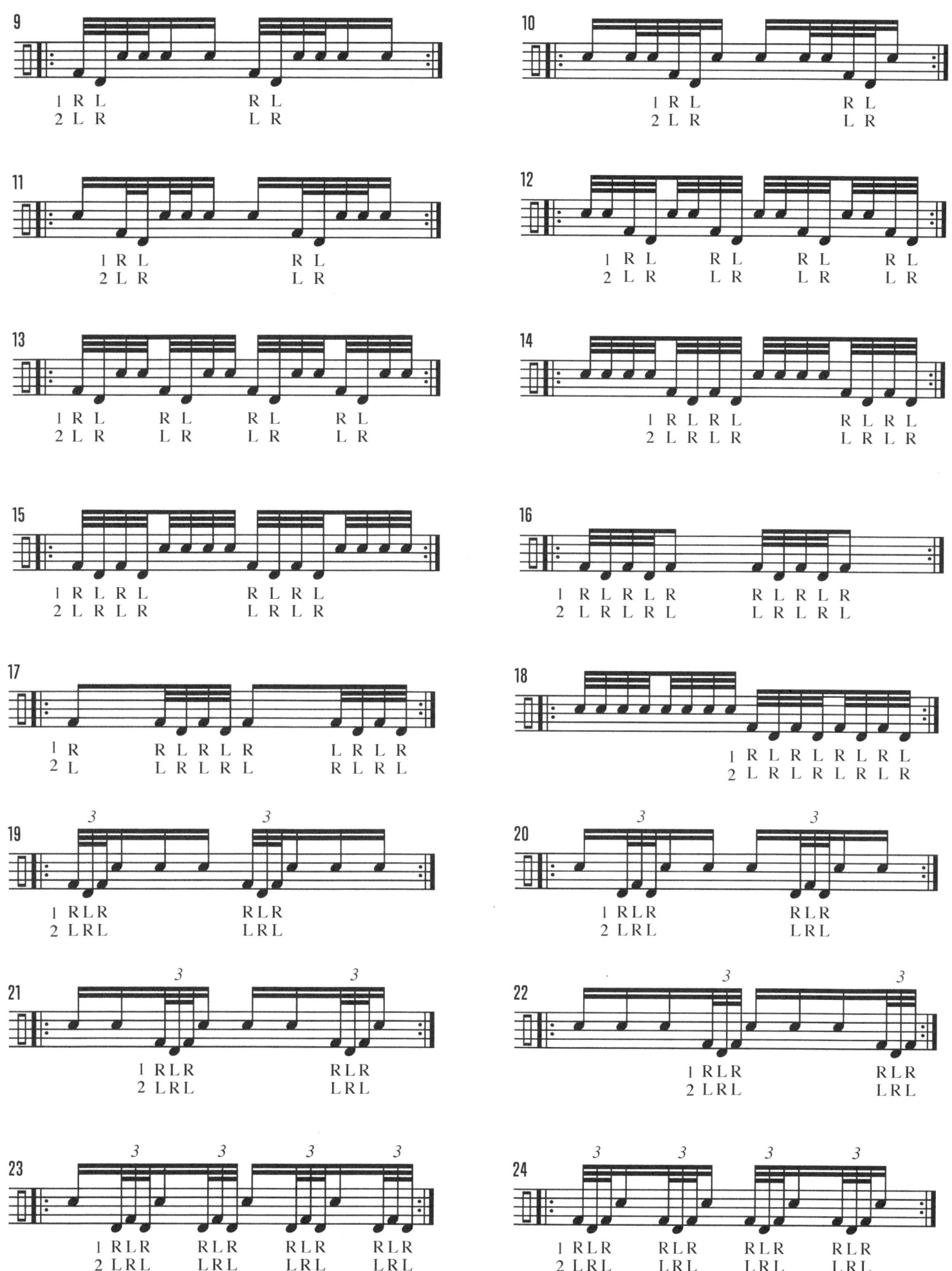

25

26

Beats

27

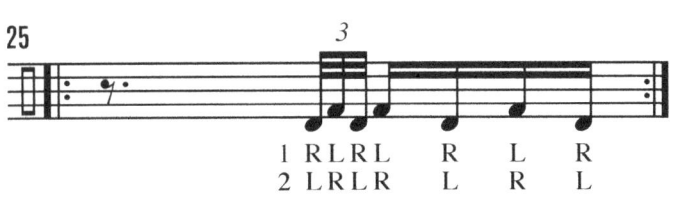

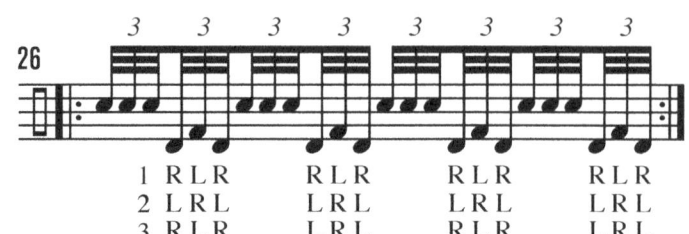

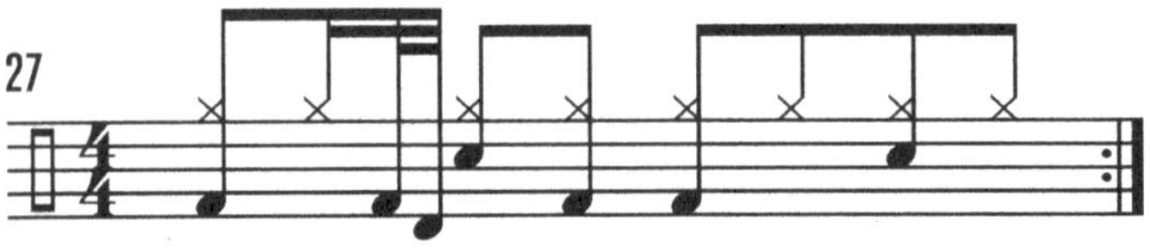

28

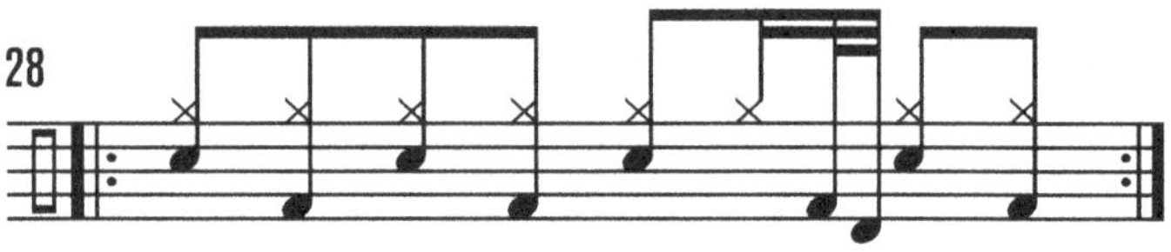

29

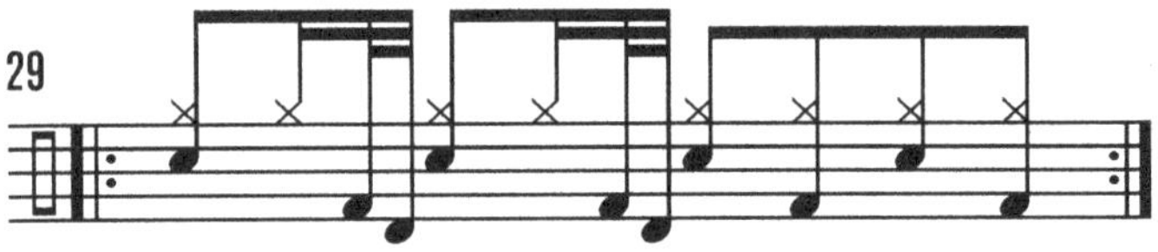

30

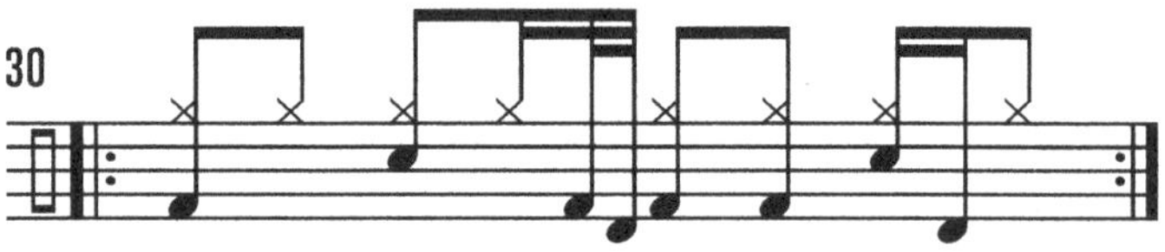

31

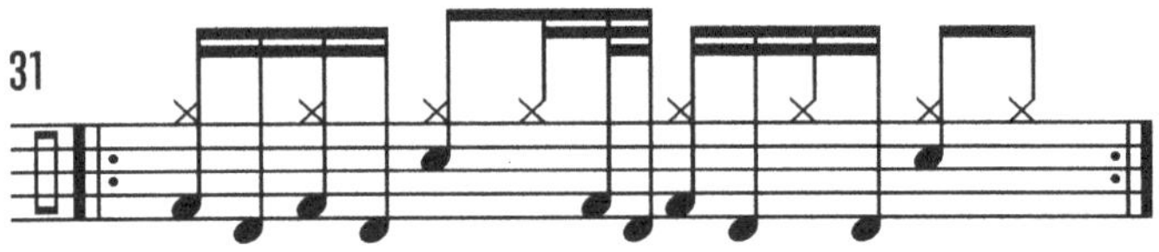

32

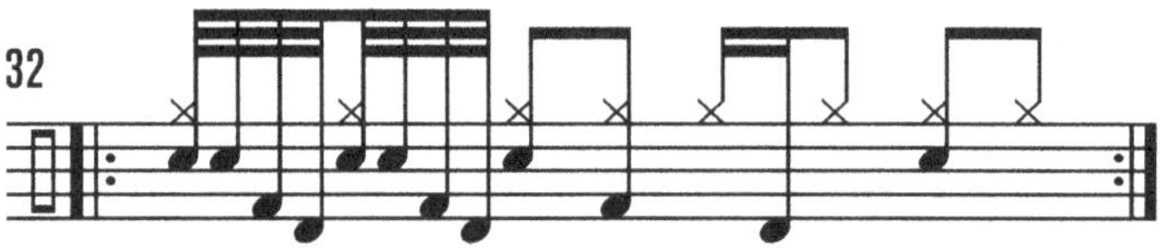

33

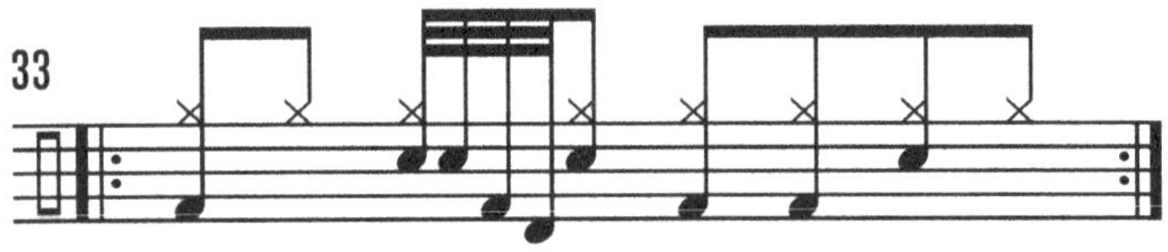

34

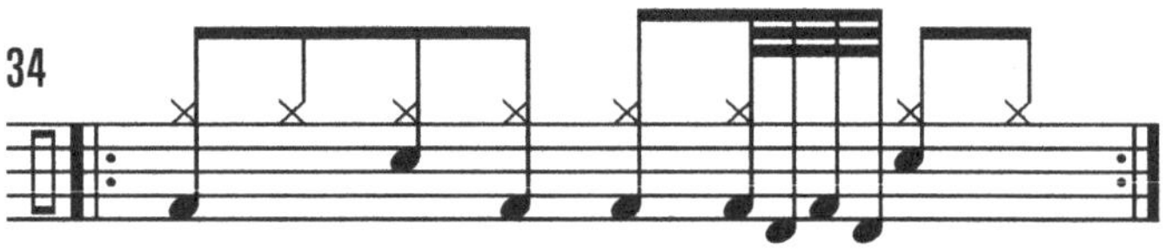

35

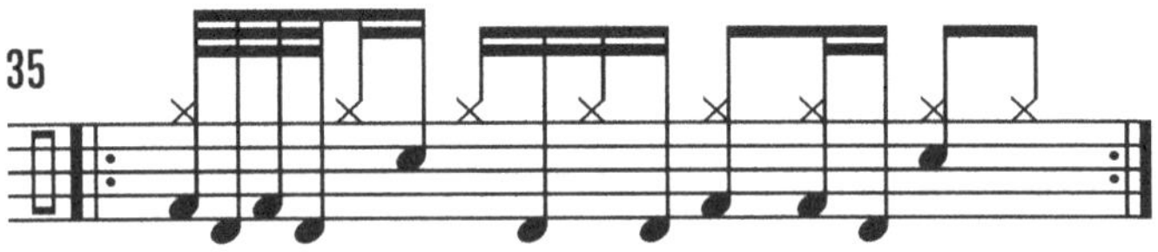

36

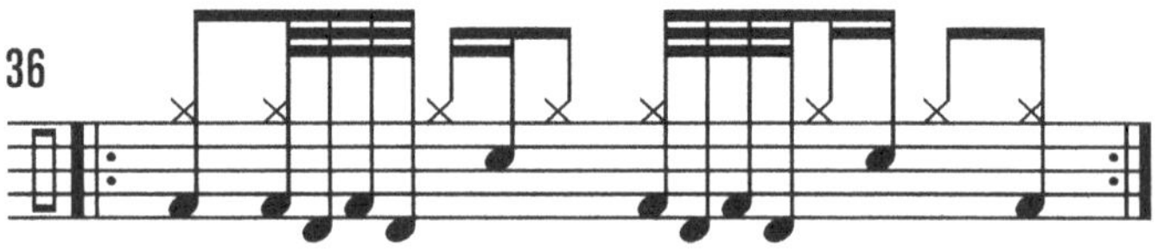

37

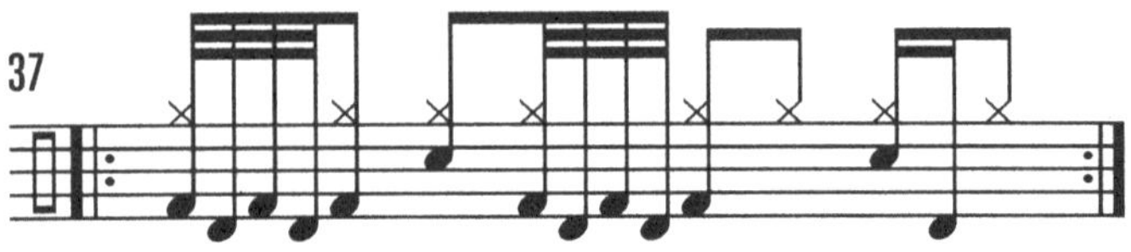

38

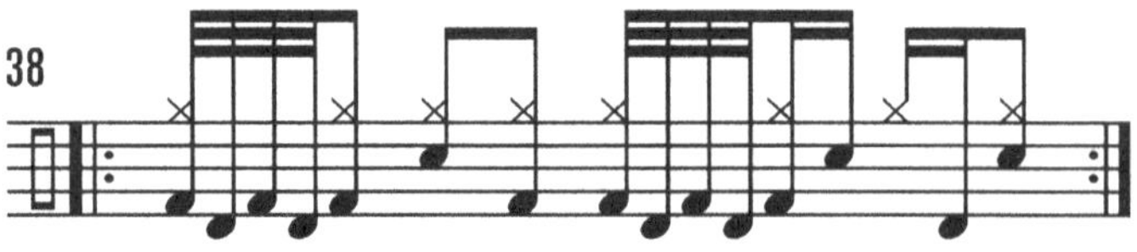

39

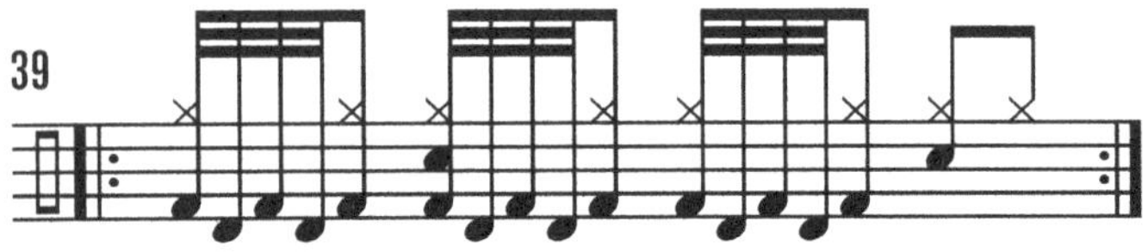

40

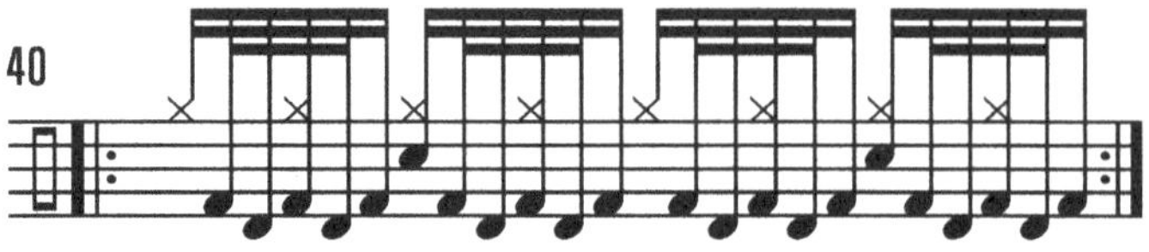

57

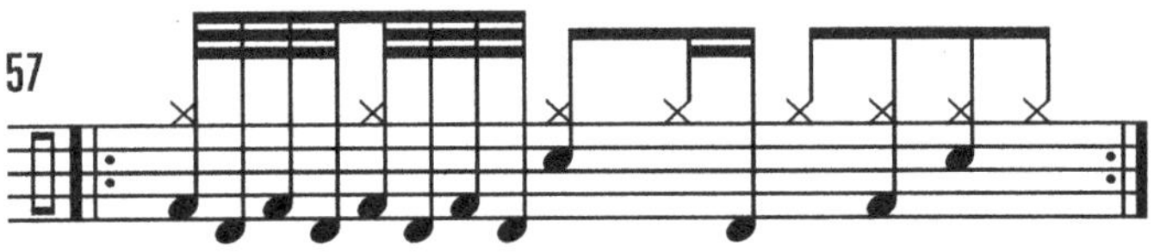

58

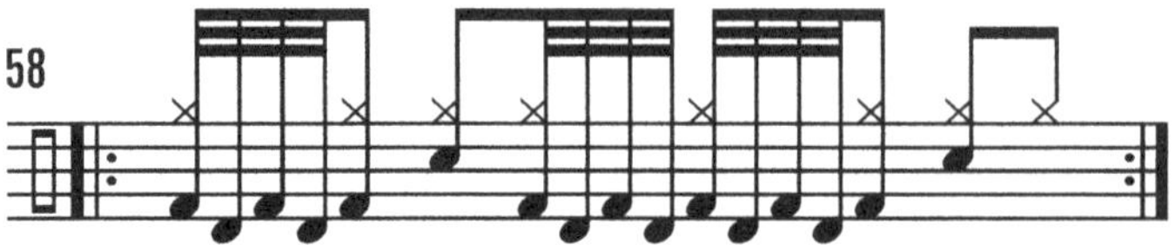

59

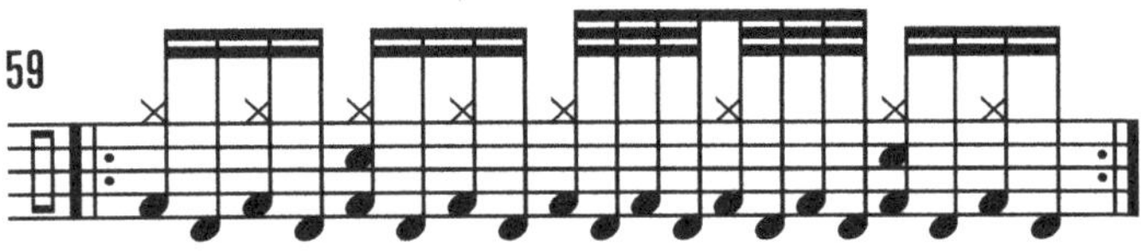

60

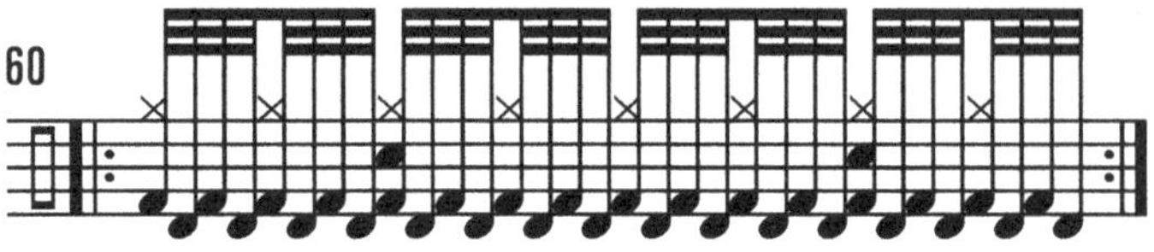

61

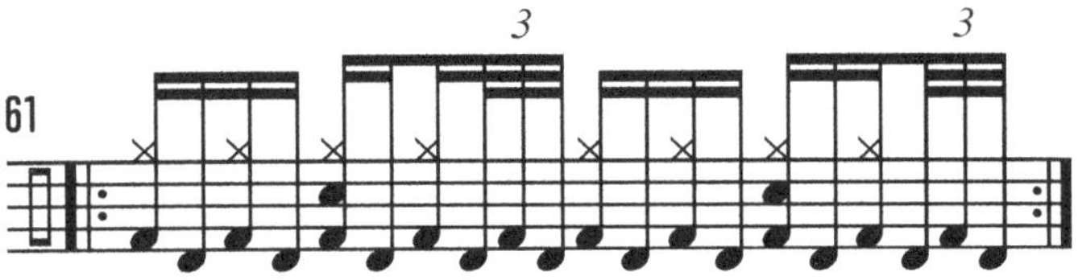

Fills

62

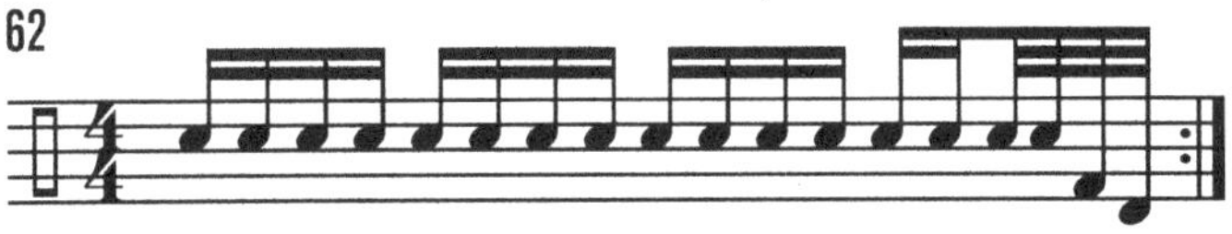

63

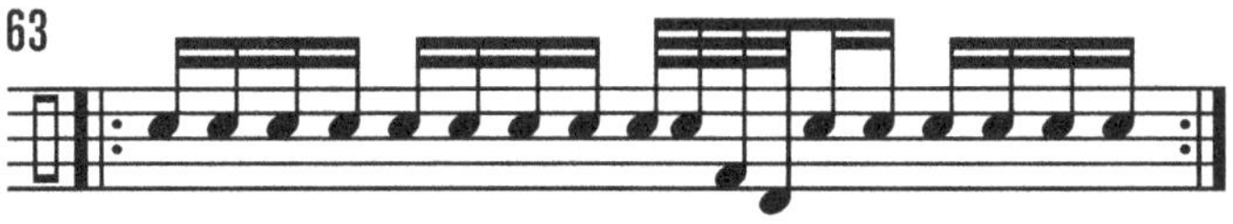

64

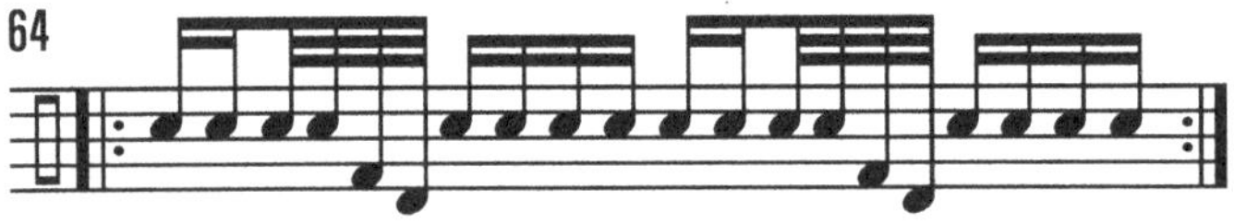

65

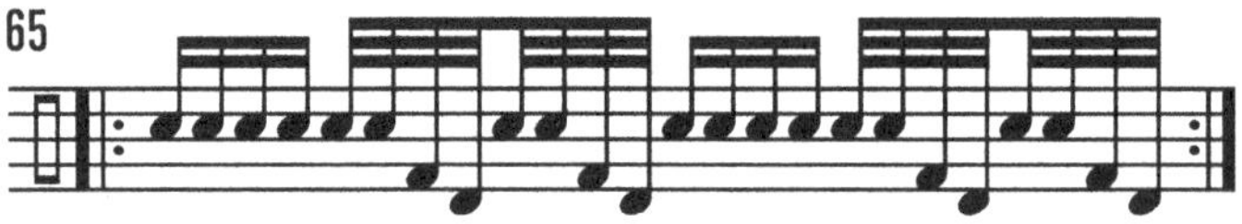

66

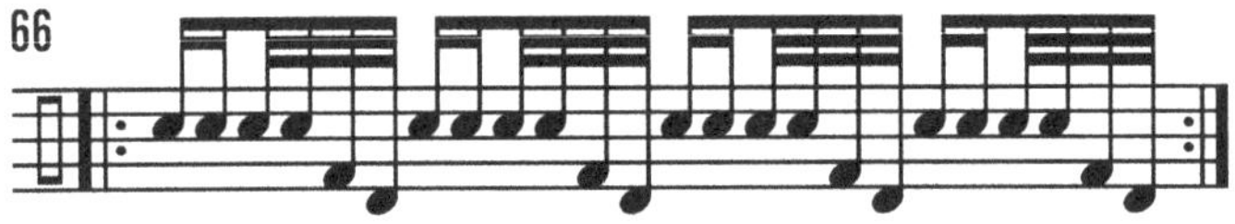

67

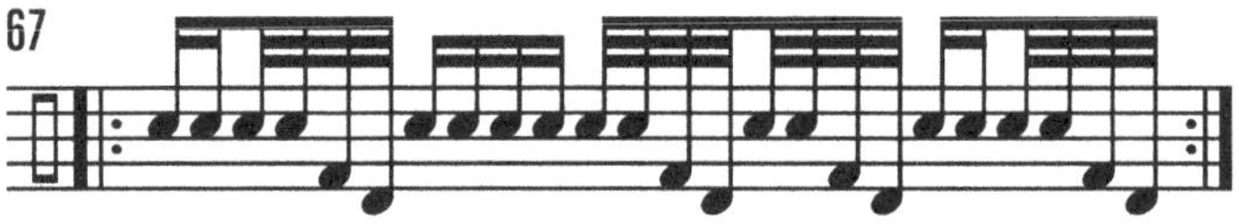

68

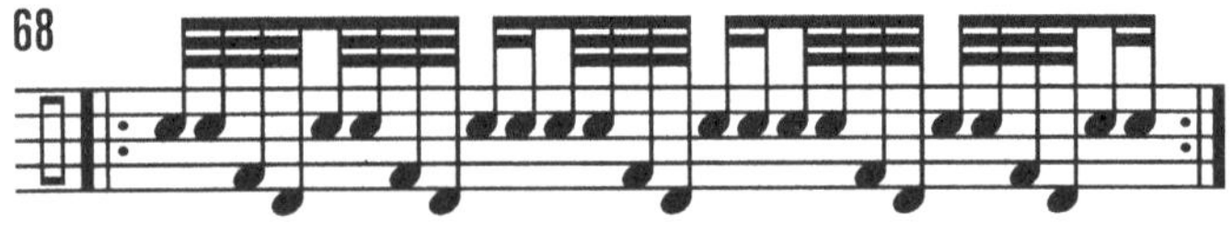

69

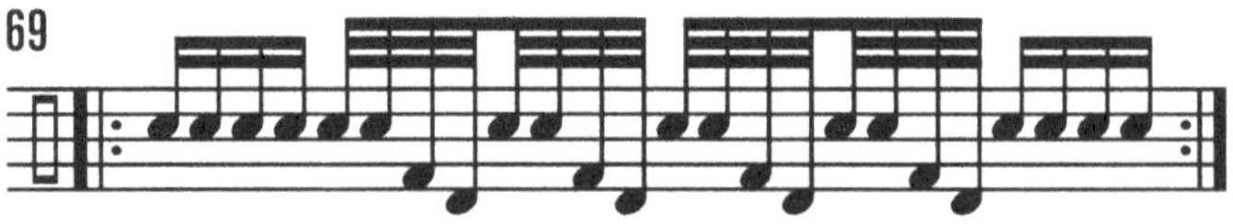

70

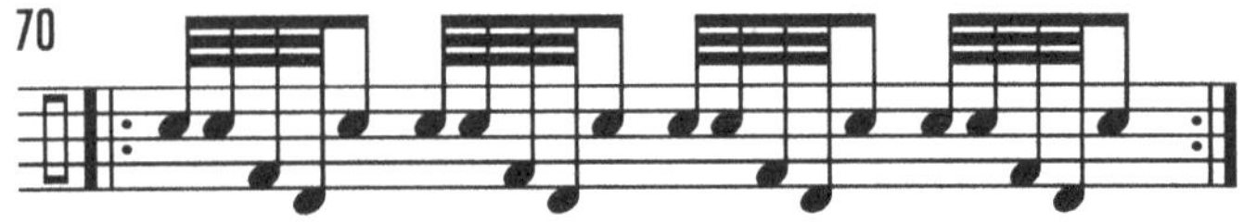

71

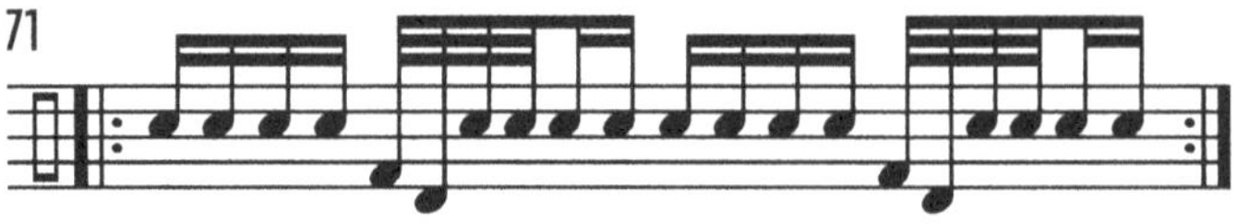

72

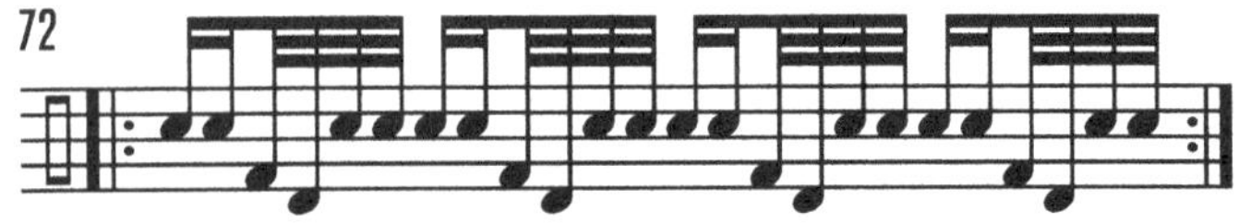

73

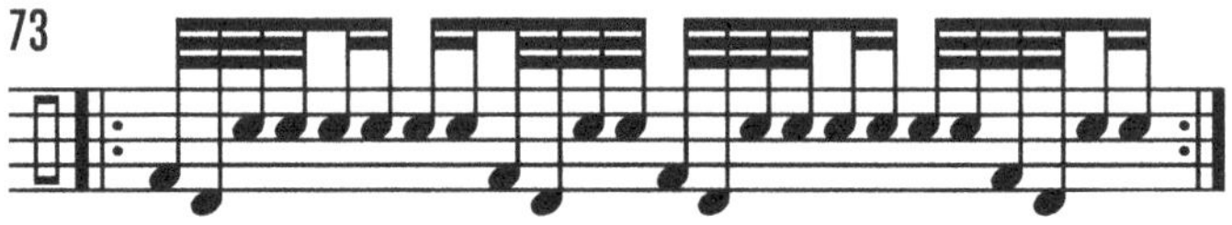

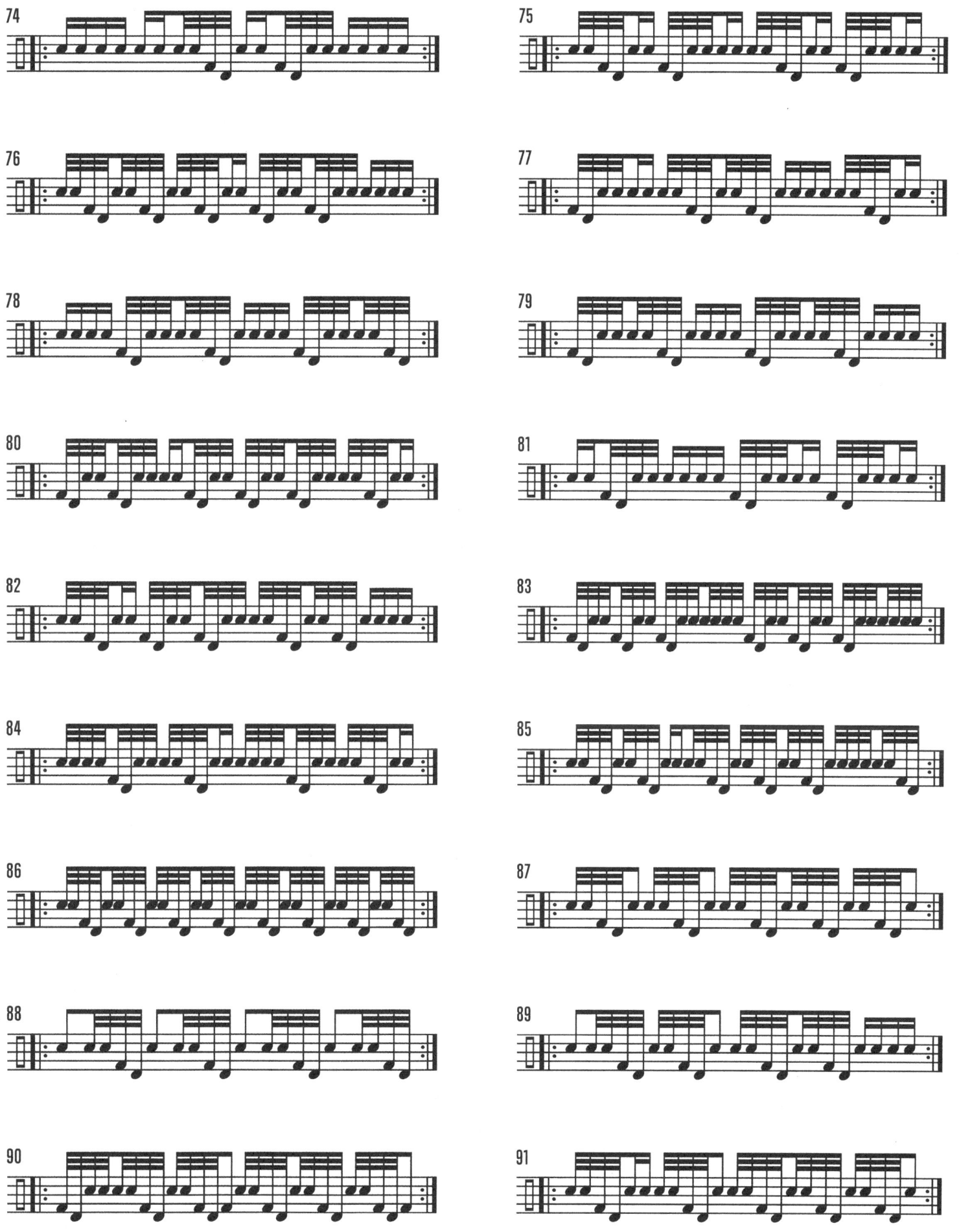

Encyclopedia Of Double Bass Drumming | 41

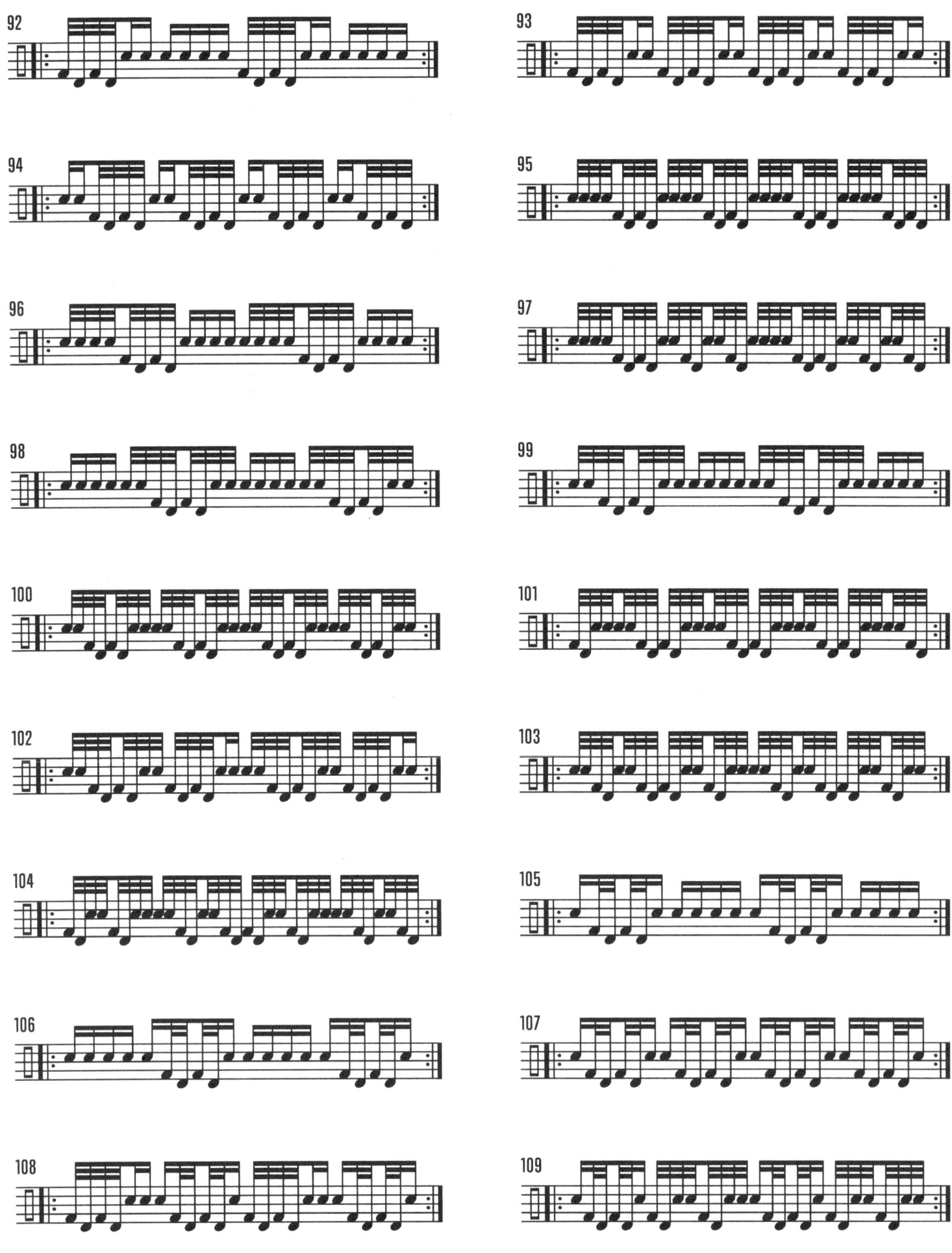

Encyclopedia Of Double Bass Drumming

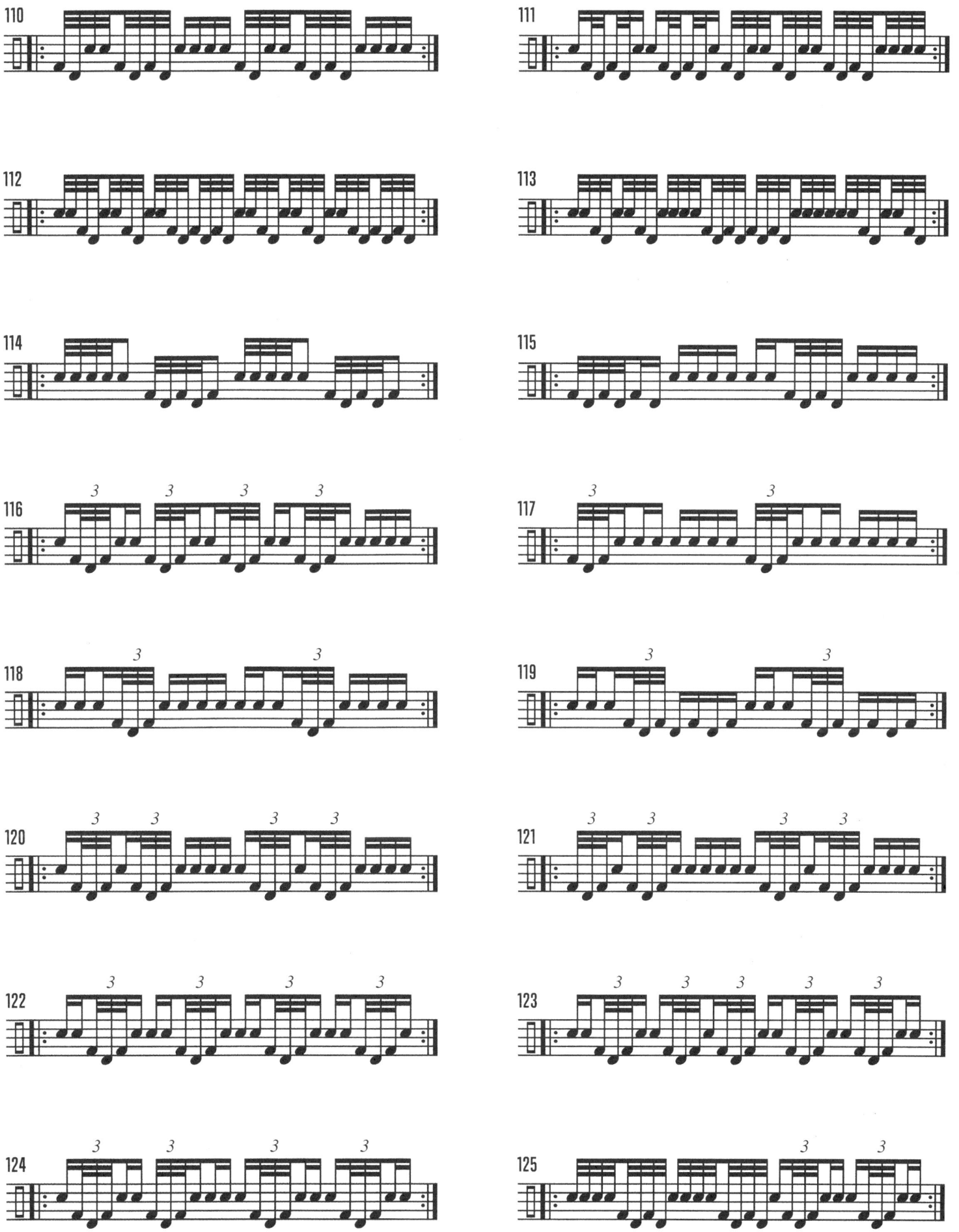

44 | Encyclopedia Of Double Bass Drumming

Chapter 9 The Blues

- This chapter will help you develop creative ways to play double bass in the blues style.
- The chapter is difficult but worth the effort.
- Practice in twelve-measure phrases, the form of traditional blues.
- Swing all 16th notes.
- Warm-up 4 alternates naturally when repeated.
- A few of the Beats and Fills don't always lead with the strong foot. Play the patterns as written and then experiment with your own footings.

Warm-Ups

Encyclopedia Of Double Bass Drumming | 45

Beats

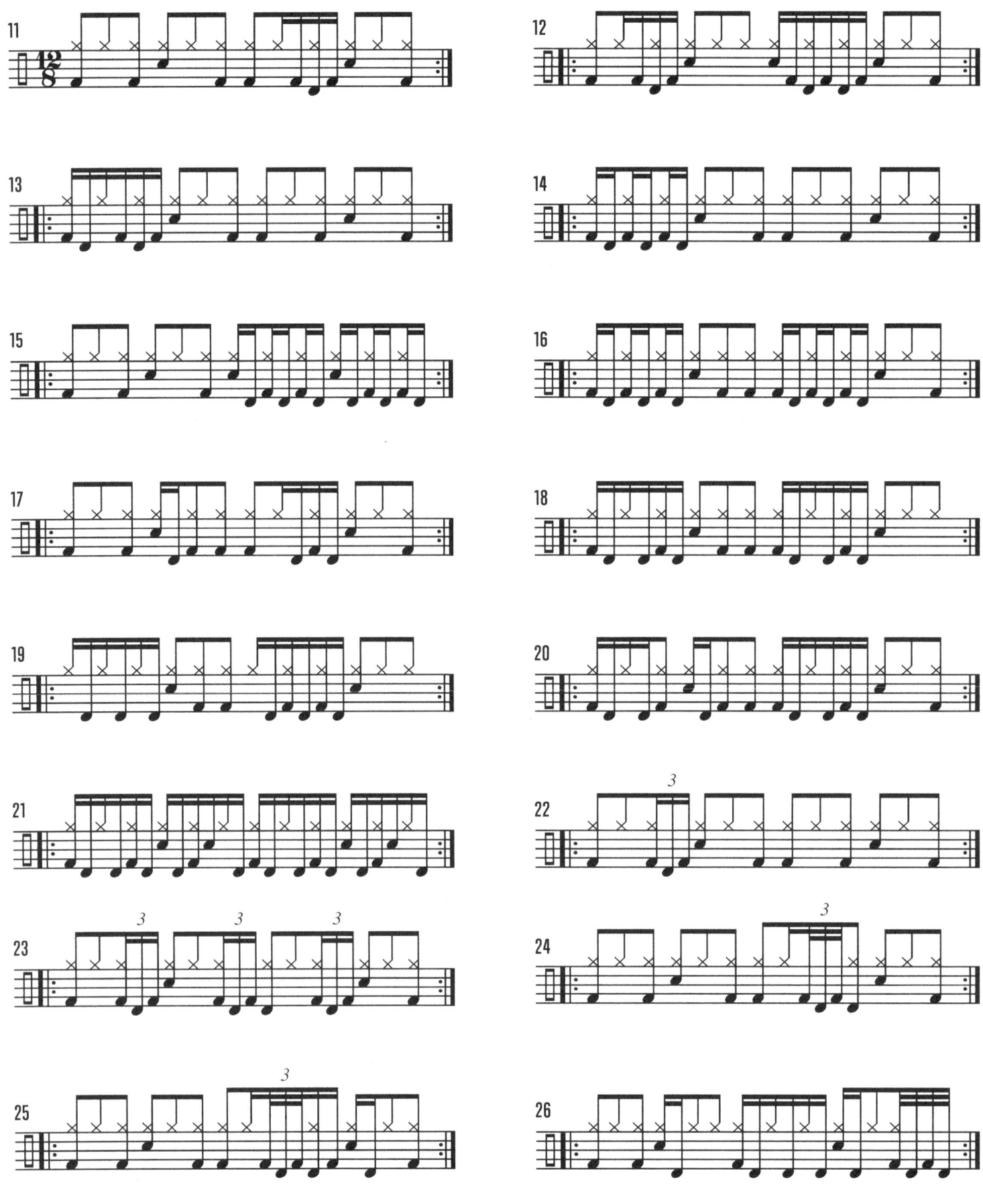

Fills

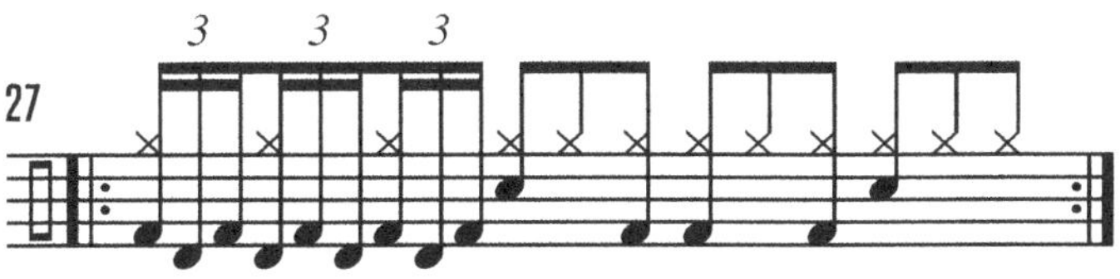

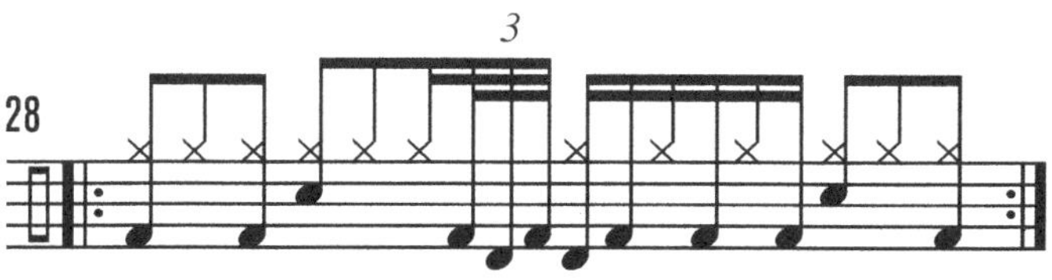

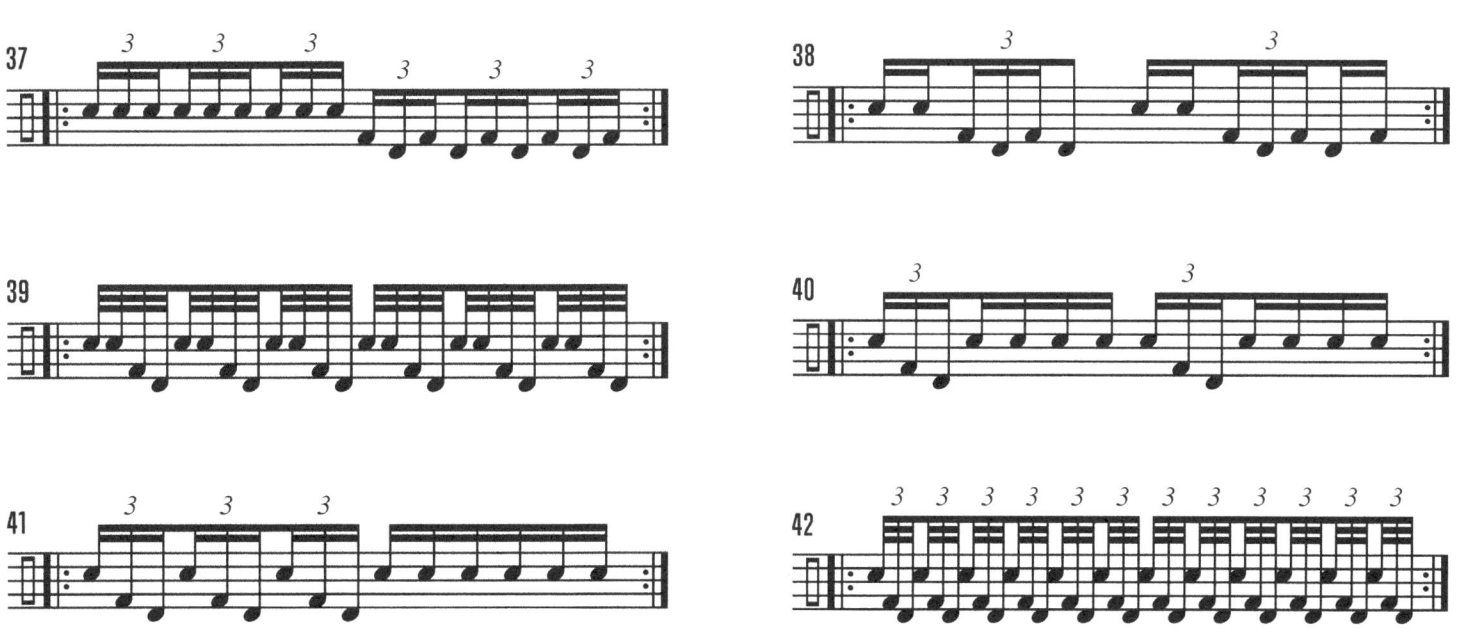

Encyclopedia Of Double Bass Drumming | 47

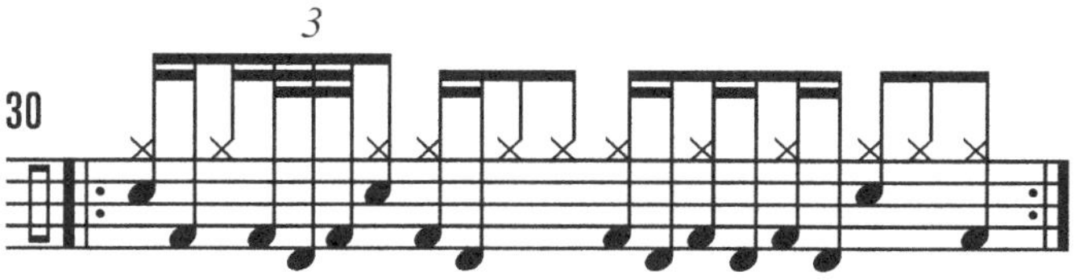

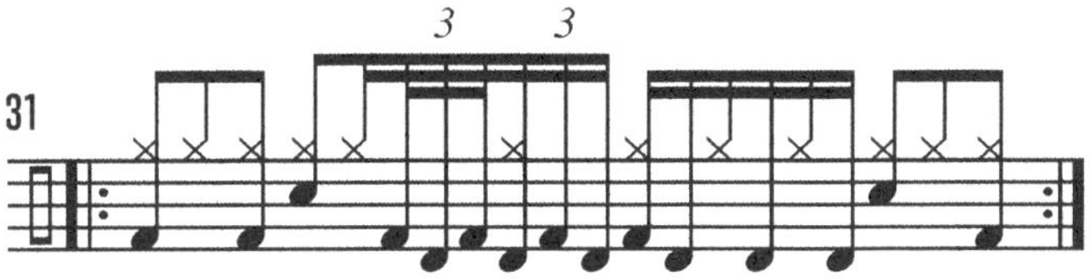

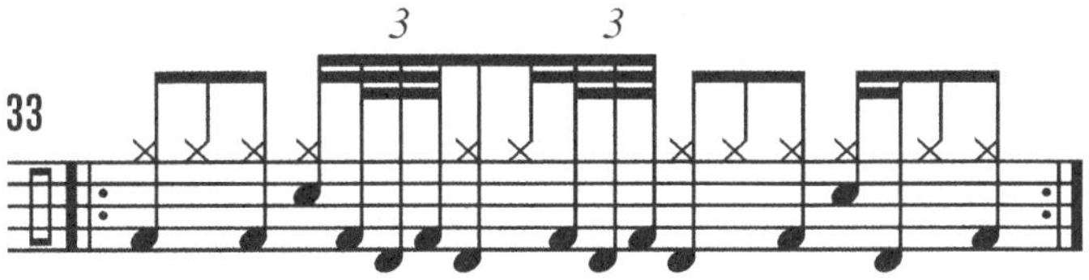

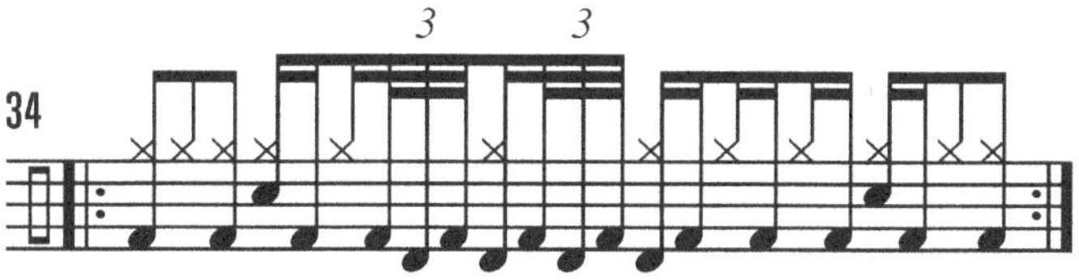

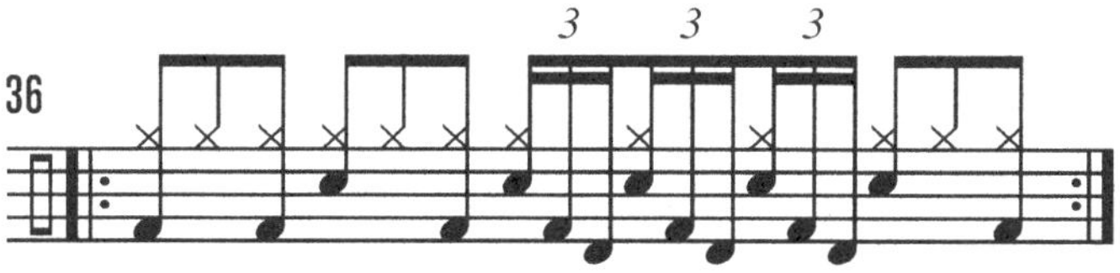

Chapter 10: 8th Notes

- 8th-note double bass is usually played at fast tempos.
- This chapter will be most helpful for beginning double bass drummers when played at slow tempos.
- The fills from the 16th-note and 8th-note triplet chapters will work great with all of the following beats.
- All beats can be played right or left foot lead.

Beats

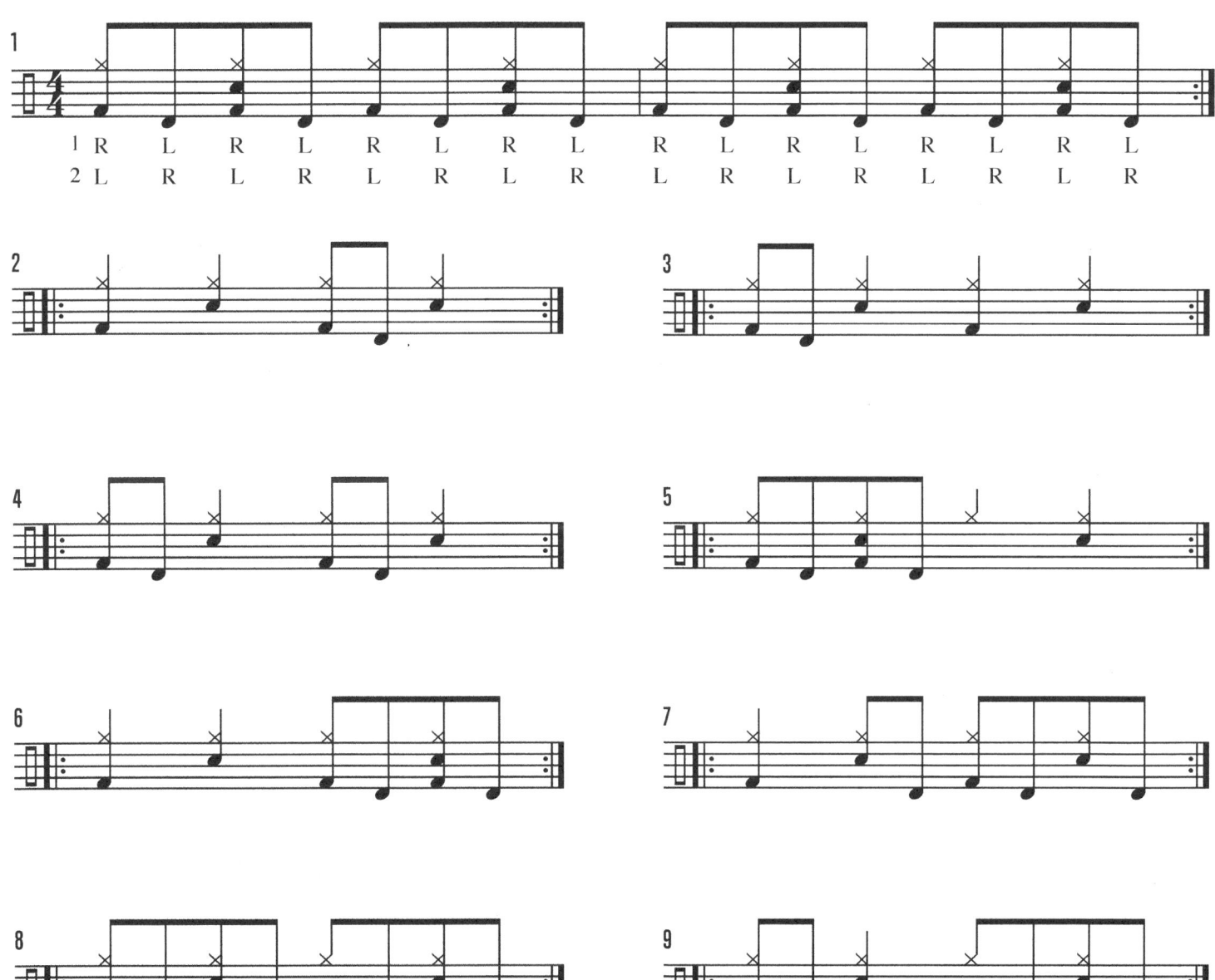

Chapter 11 Power Threes

- Power threes are a quick and effective way to develop a thick-sounding beat.
- The feet stay constant in either a straight or shuffle rhythm, while the left hand (on a snare or tom) plays between the rhythm of the feet.
- In Beats 1–5 the feet must be played consistently in a straight-8th note feel.
- Beats 6–10 are in a triplet or shuffle feel.
- Try the power threes playing 16th notes in your feet
- Remember to try different footings. See what works for you.

Beats

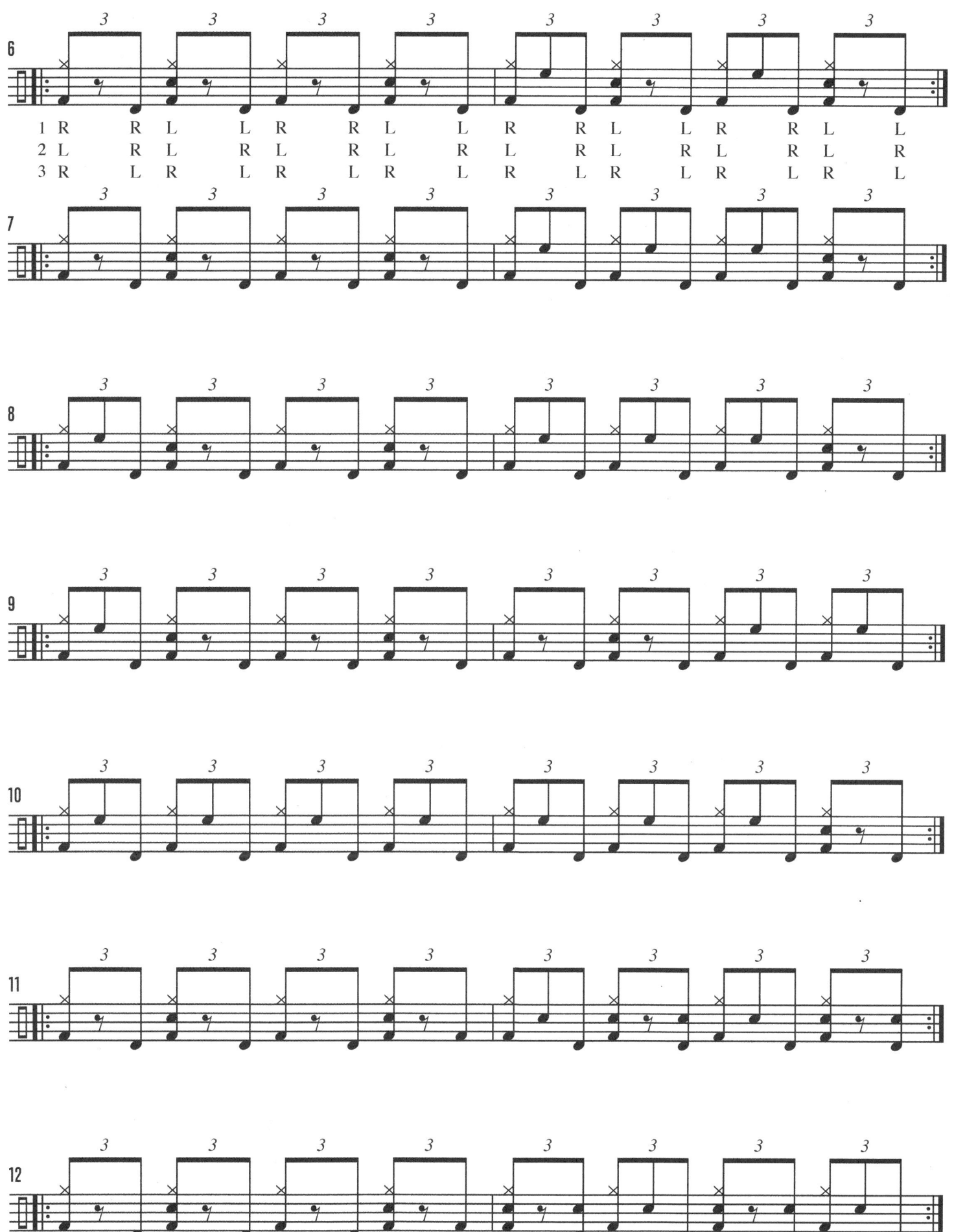

Chapter 12 Linear Cross-Rhythms

- This chapter will help you develop linear double bass fills.
- The linear concept is simply this—none of your limbs hit at the same time.
- Cross-rhythms are usually odd groupings of notes (3, 5, 6, 7, 9) that are played repetitively and do not coincide with the downbeats of even-note groupings. It's possible to have even-note cross-rhythms (see Triplet 4's on page 65).
- All of the fills in this chapter utilize linear cross-rhythms.
- Orchestrate your hands between the snare and toms.
- On most of the fills, playing one hand on a tom sounds great.
- Experiment with your own melodic combinations.
- All bass drum rhythms can be played in unison with your hands playing cymbals. Although the patterns then are no longer linear, they are still cross-rhythms and sound terrific.

3/16 Grouping Warm-Ups

- Practice the grouping warm-ups first before applying them in one- or two-bar phrases.
- Certain linear cross-rhythms include one possible sticking. Feel free to come up with your own.

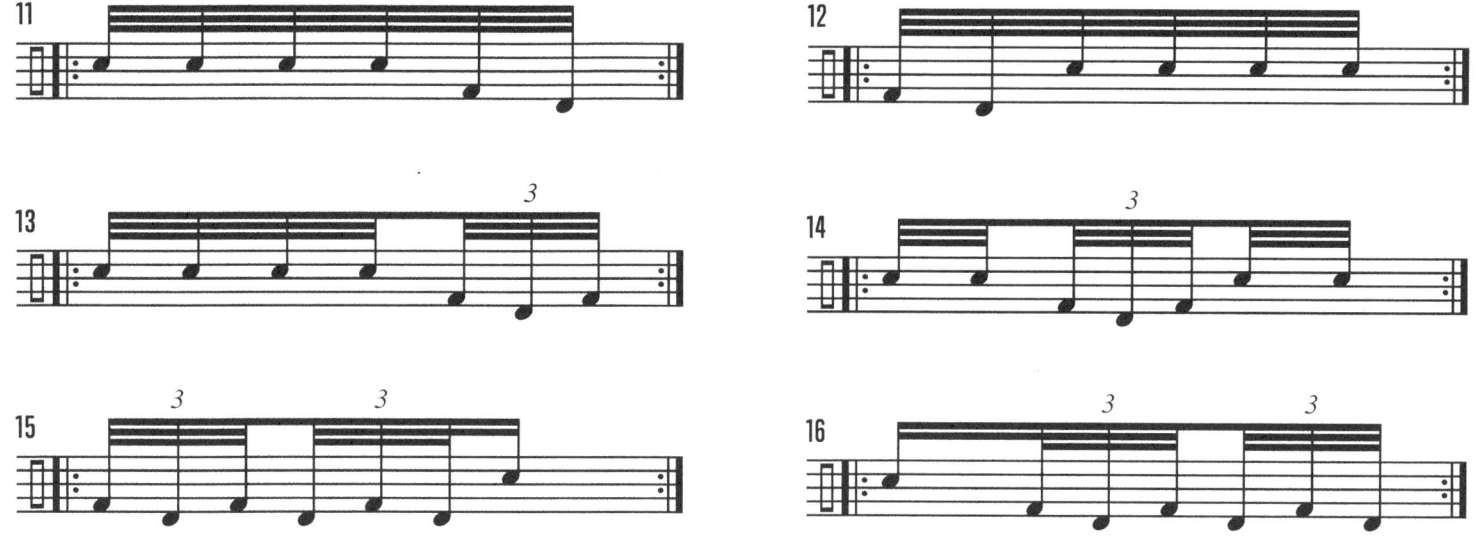

Three-Note Rhythms

- A three-note linear cross-rhythm can consist of just three 16th notes or any rhythm that can fit into the space of three notes.

- This same cross-rhythmic approach applies to fives, sevens, and nines, or triplet fours, fives, and sevens.

Encyclopedia Of Double Bass Drumming | 55

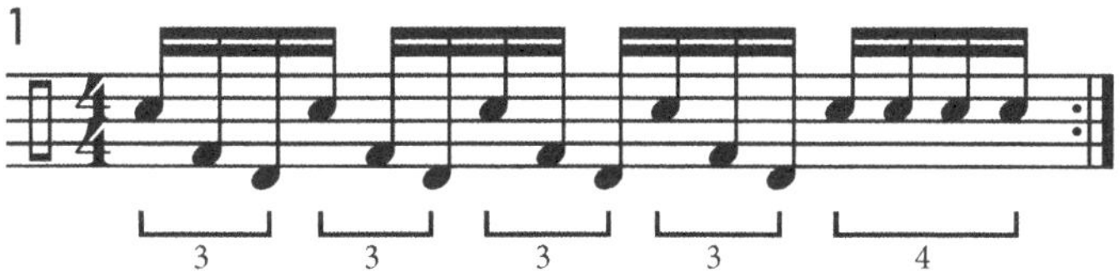

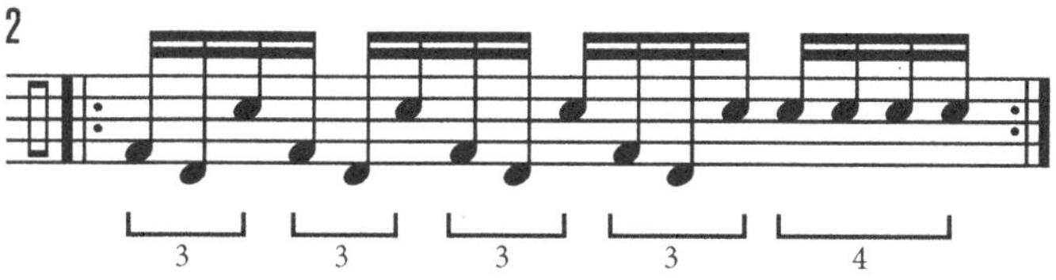

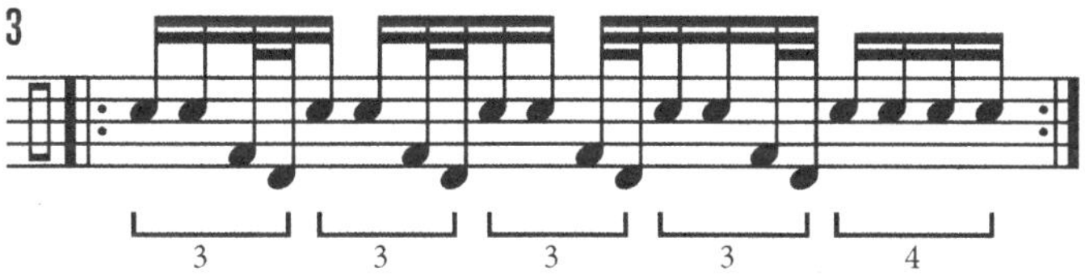

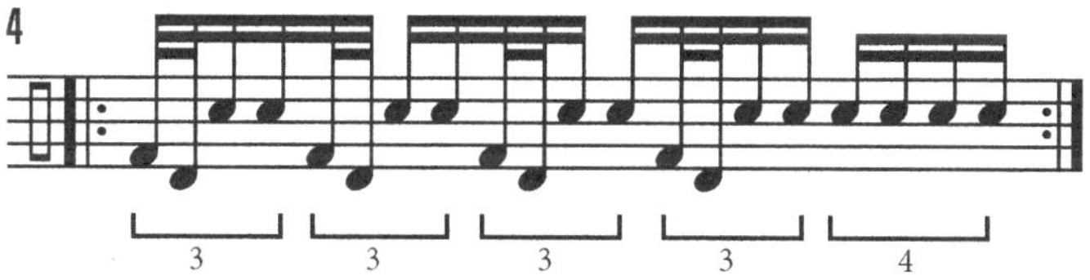

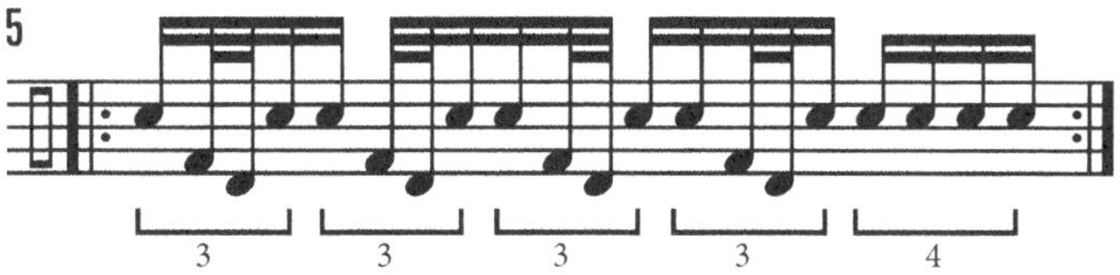

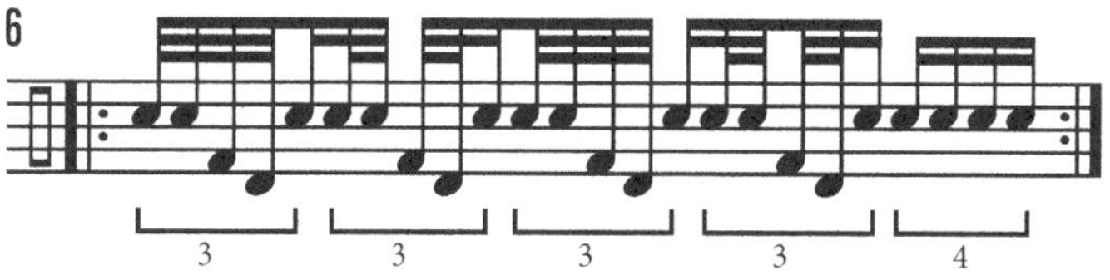

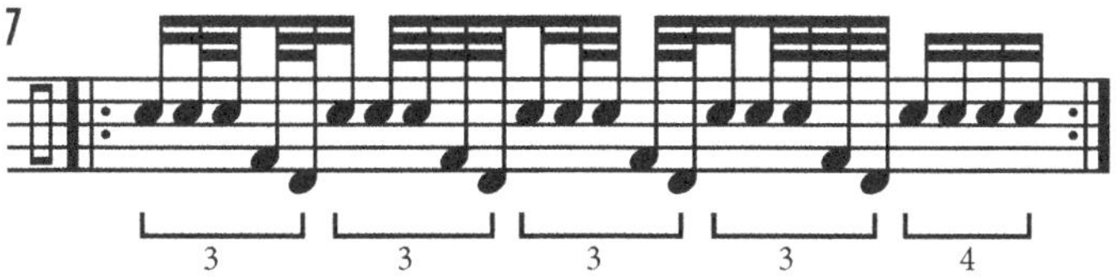

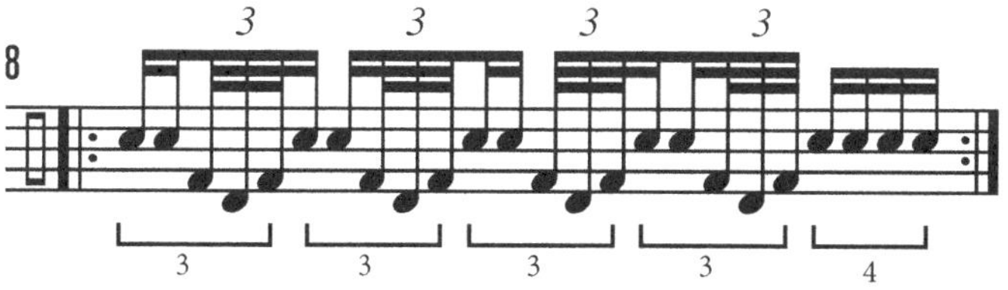

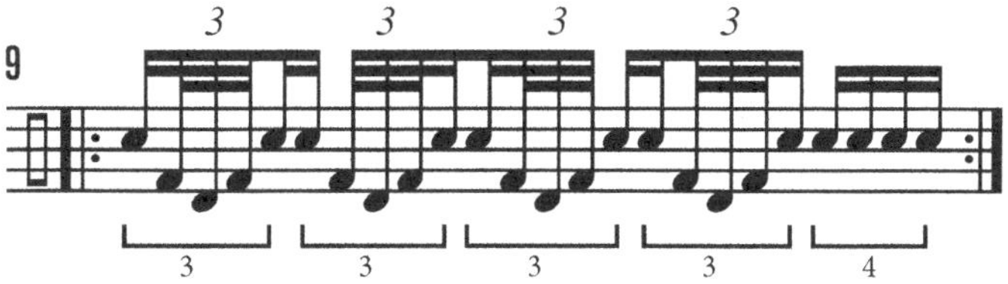

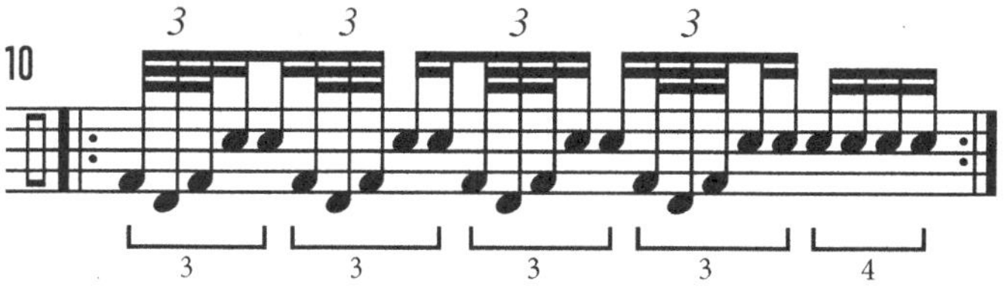

11

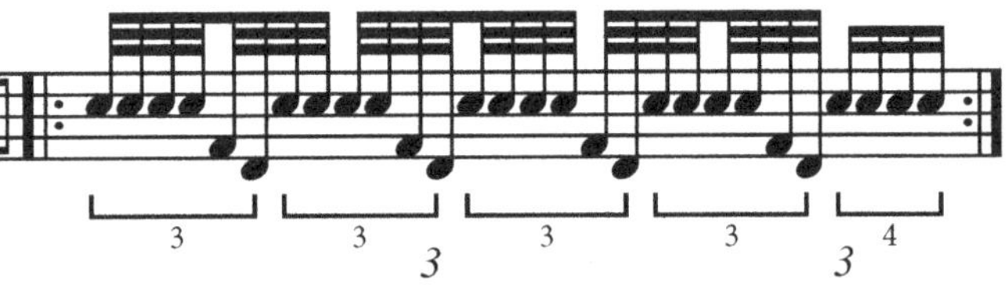

12

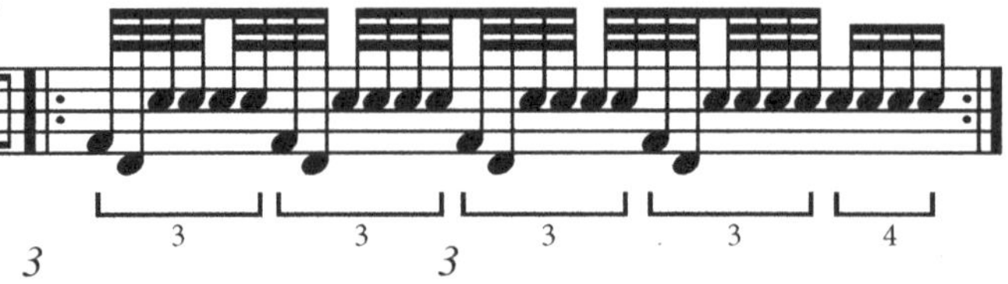

13

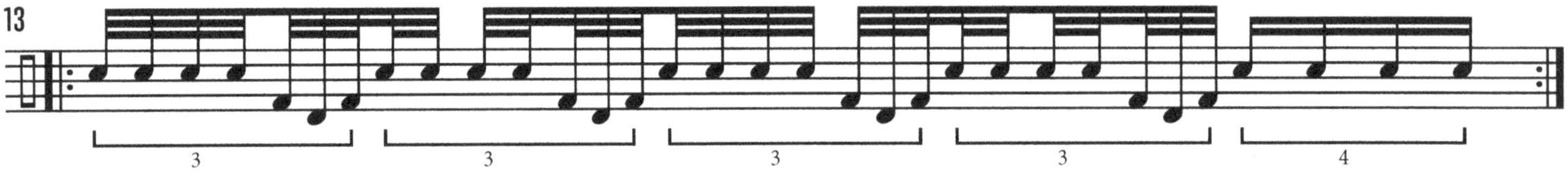

14

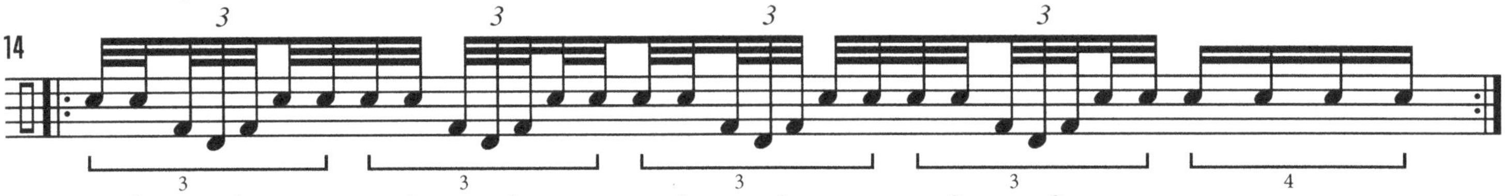

15

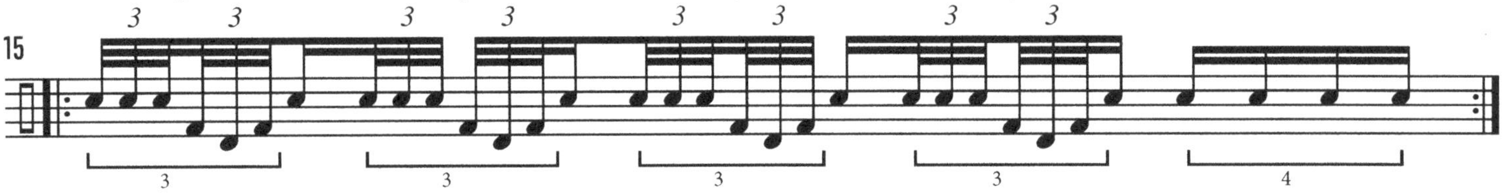

16

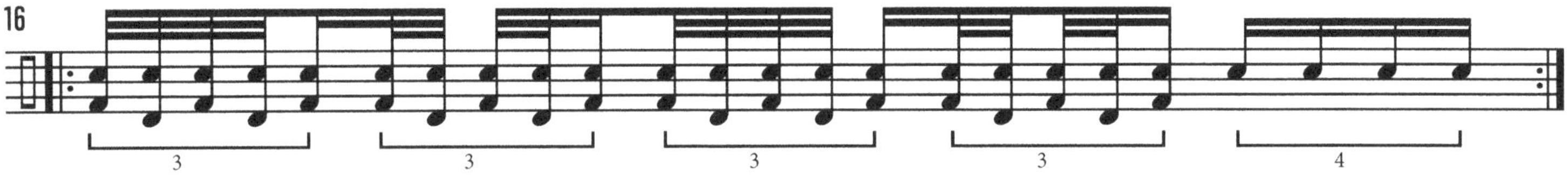

5/16 Grouping Warm-Ups

1

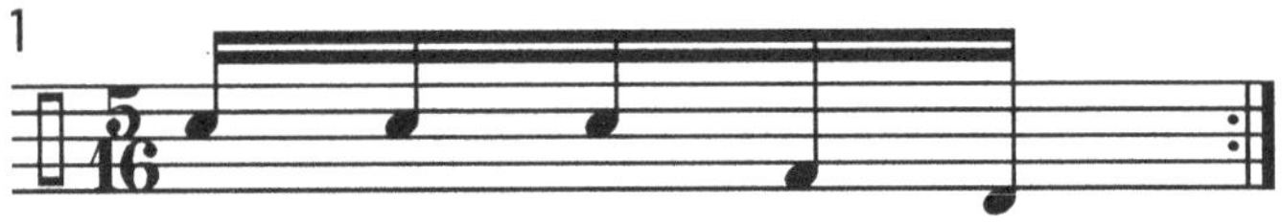

2

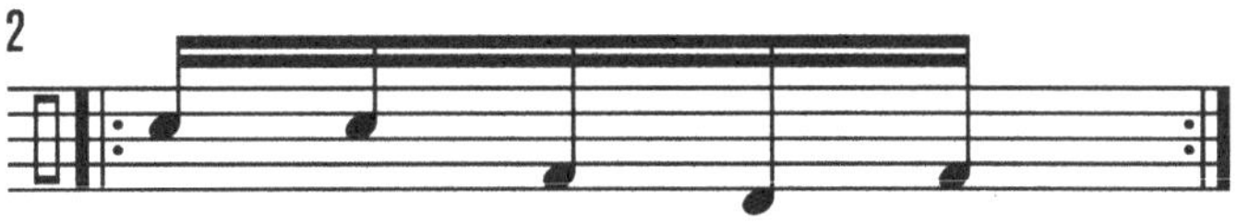

3

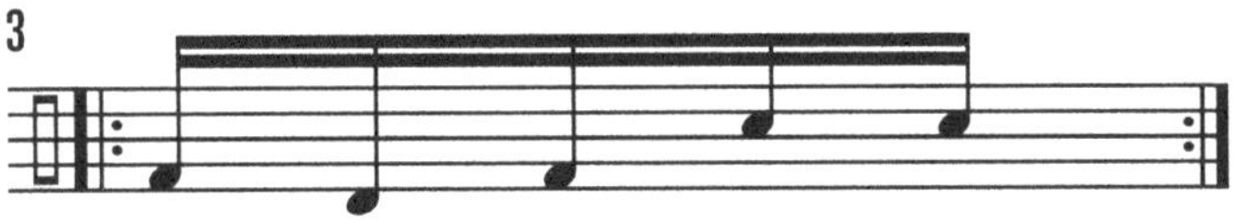

4

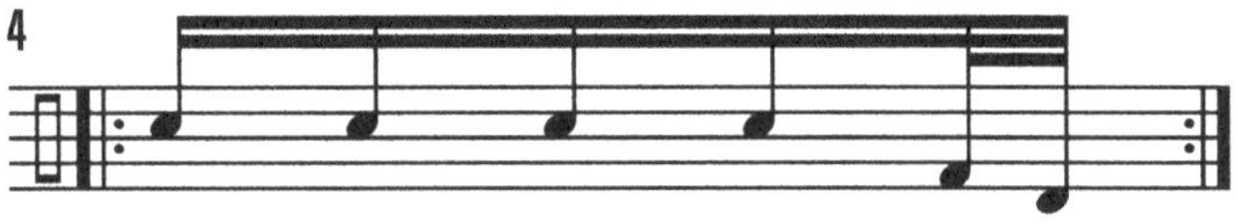

5

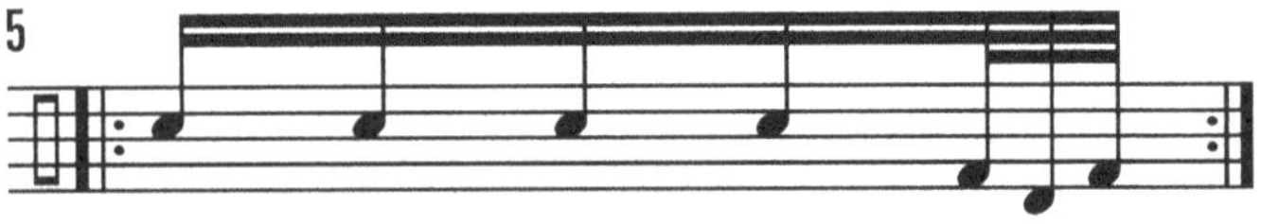

6

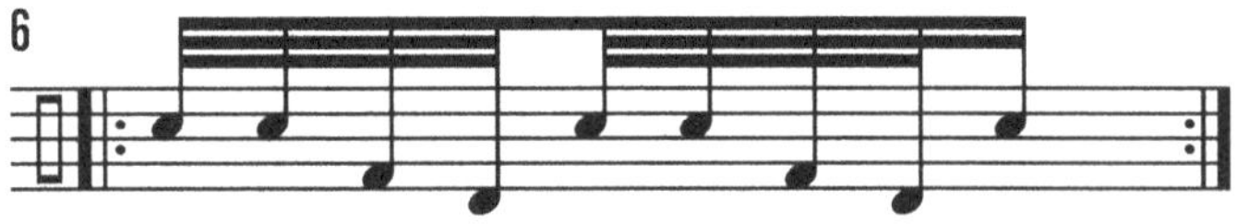

7

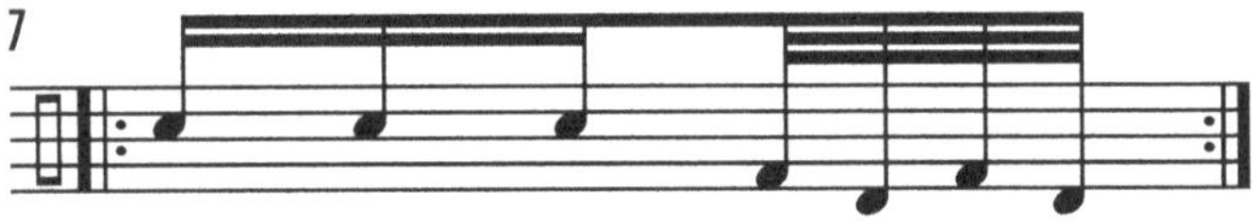

8

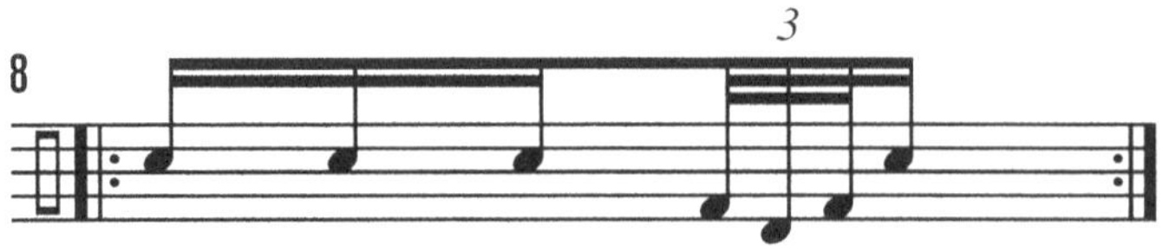

9

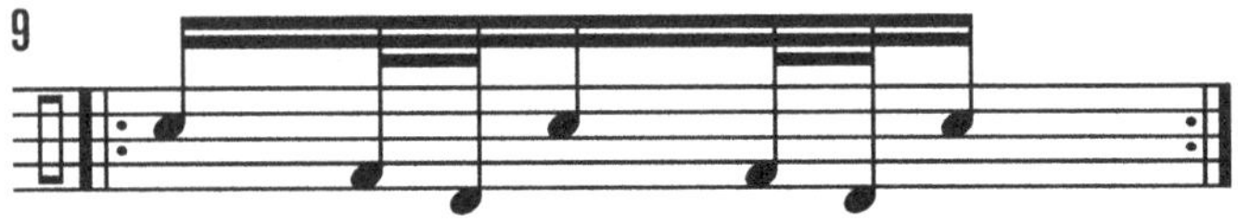

10

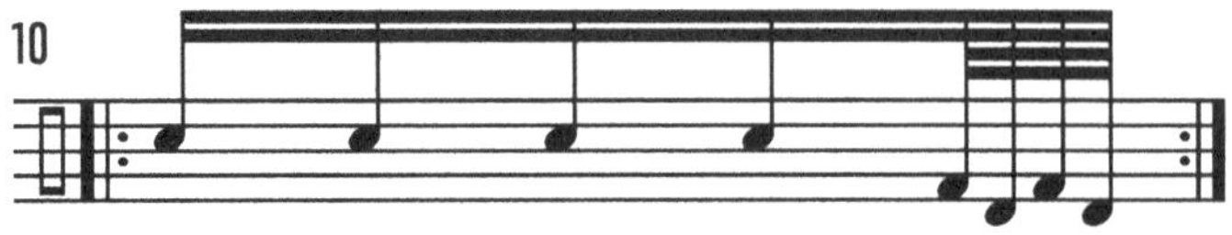

Five-Note Linear Cross Rhythms

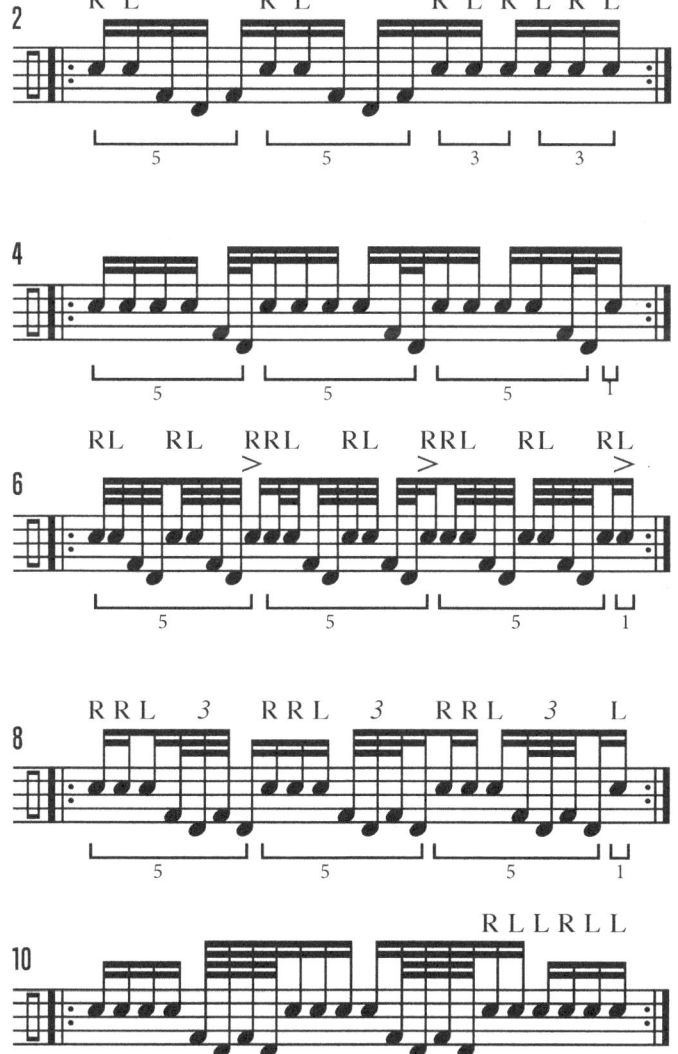

6/16 Grouping Warm-Ups

Encyclopedia Of Double Bass Drumming

9

10

11

12

13

14

Six-Note Linear Cross Rhythms

1
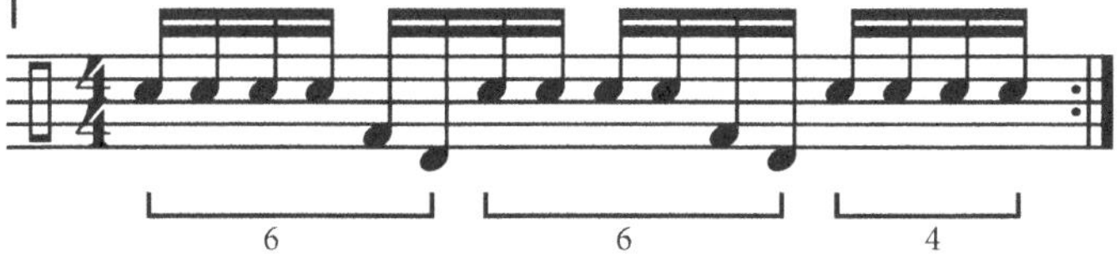

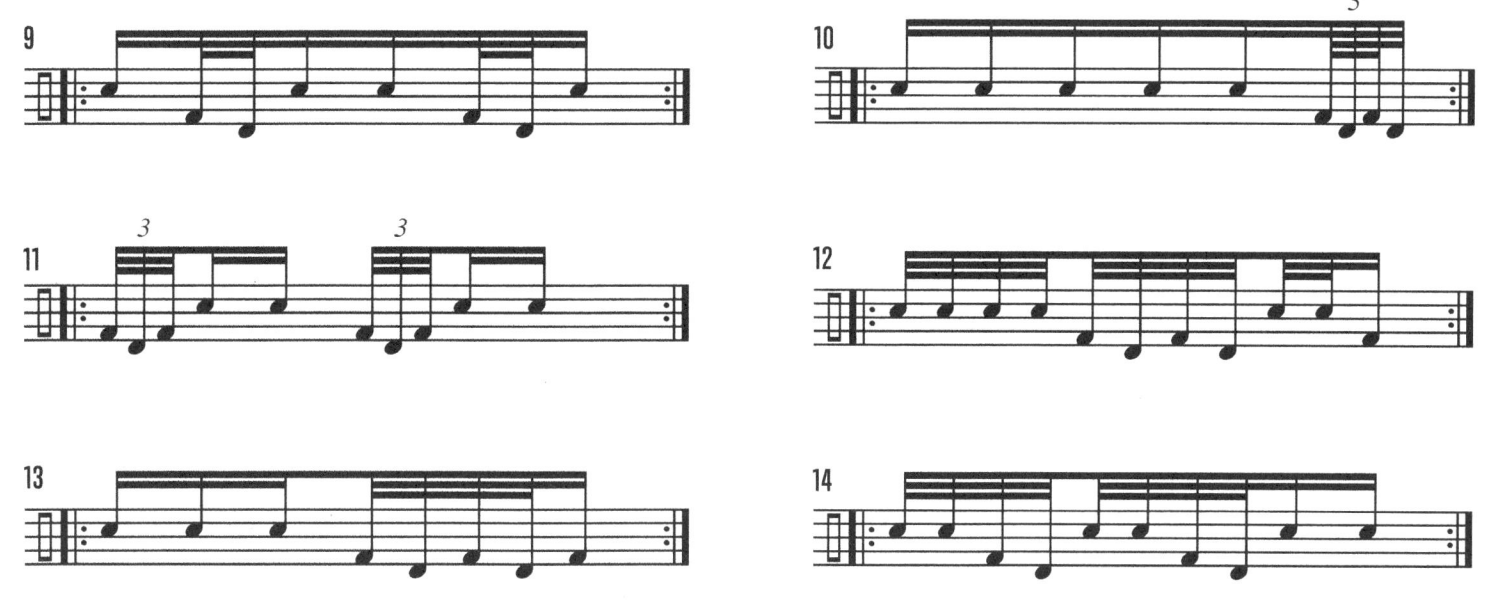

2
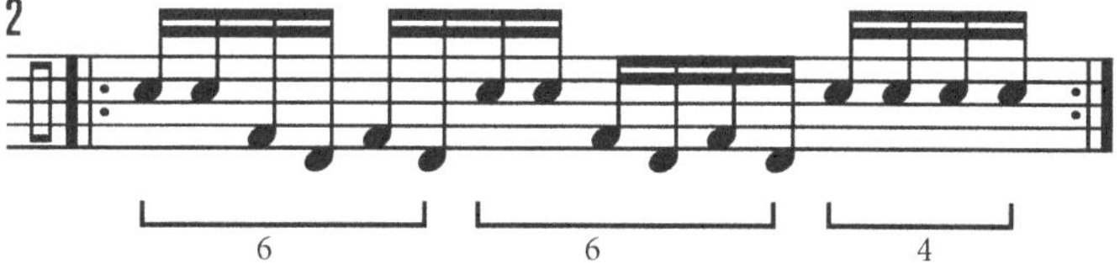

3
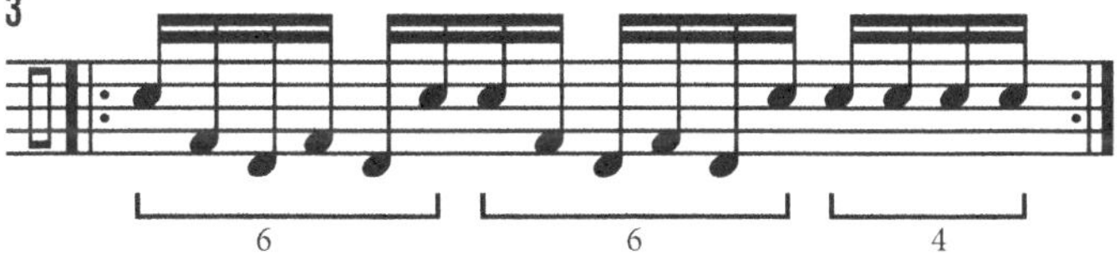

4
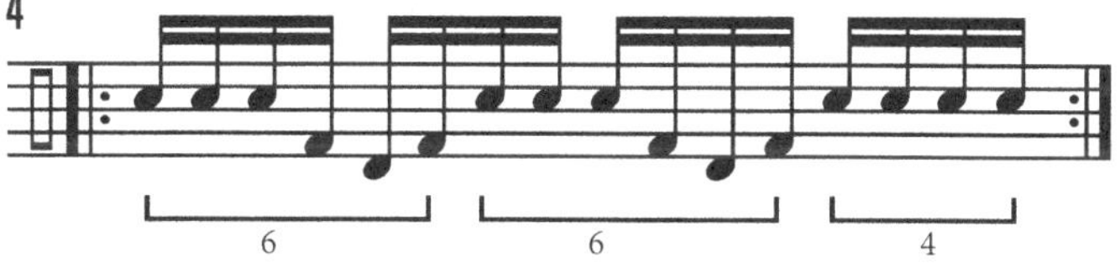

5
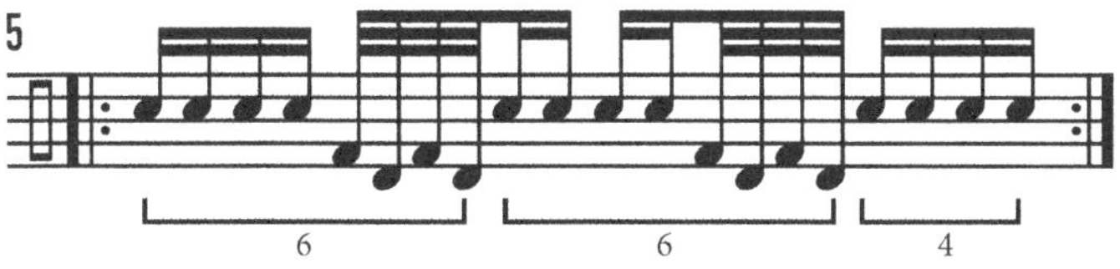

6
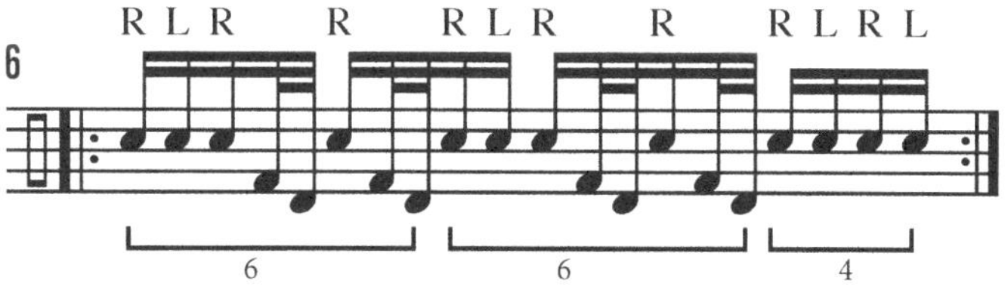

7
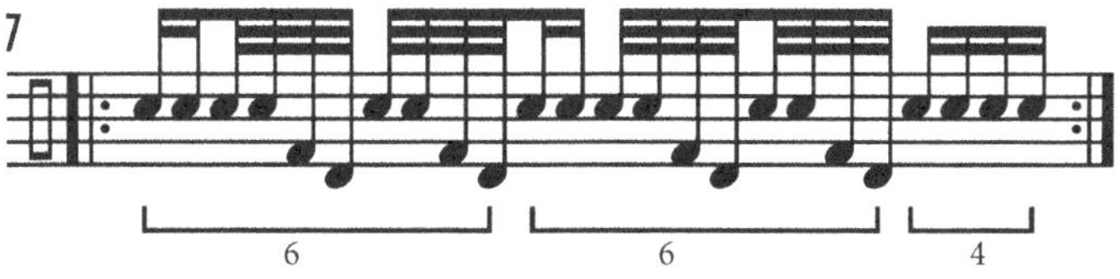

8
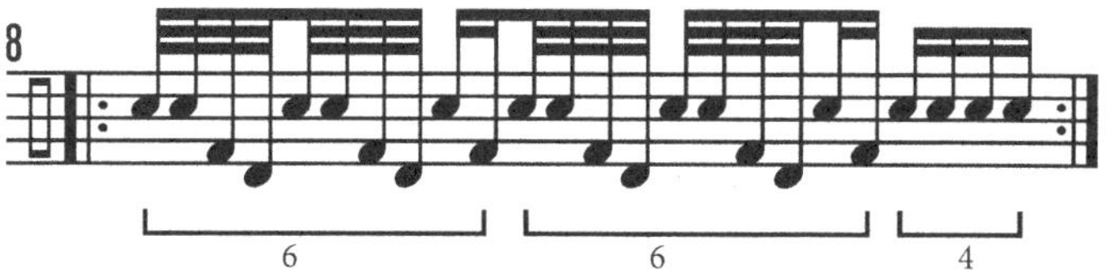

9
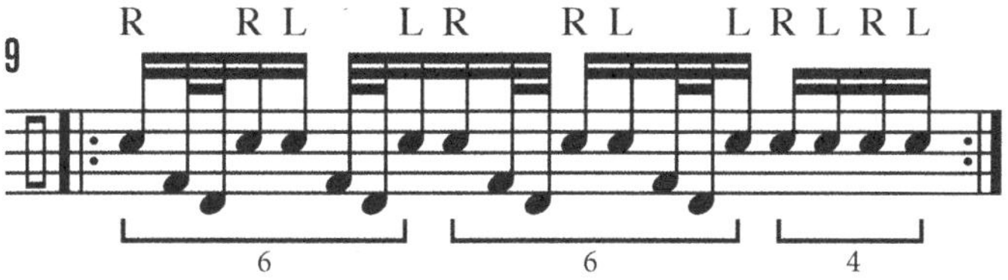

10
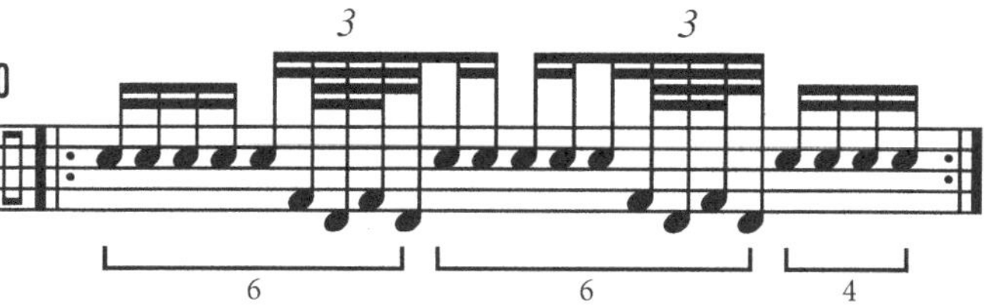

7/16 Grouping Warm-Ups

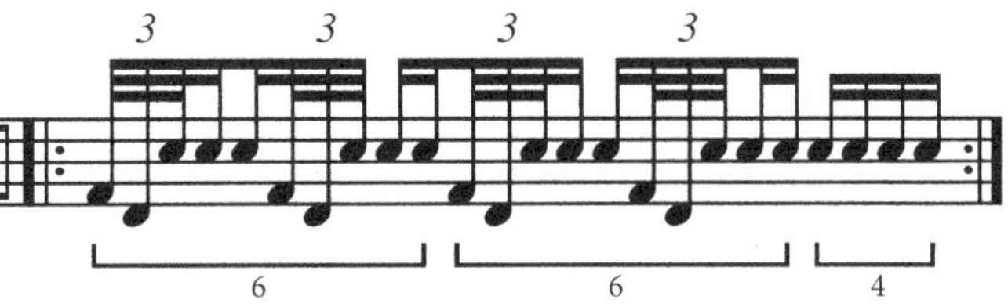

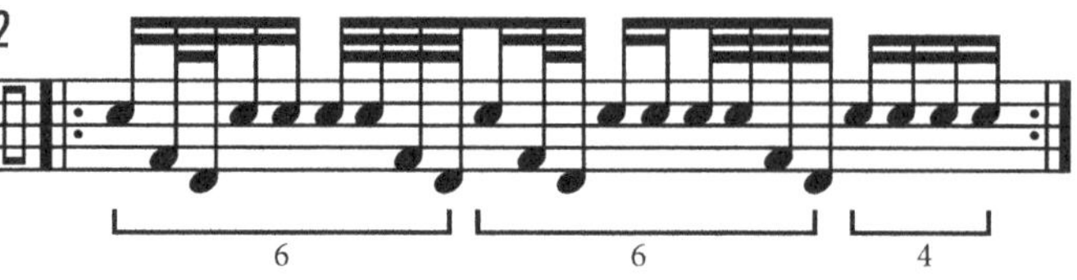

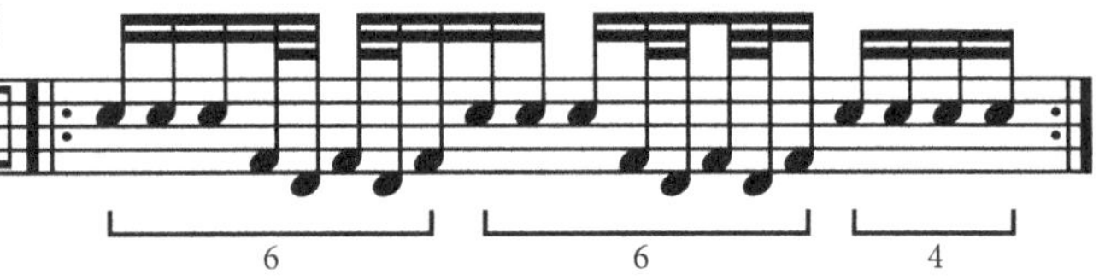

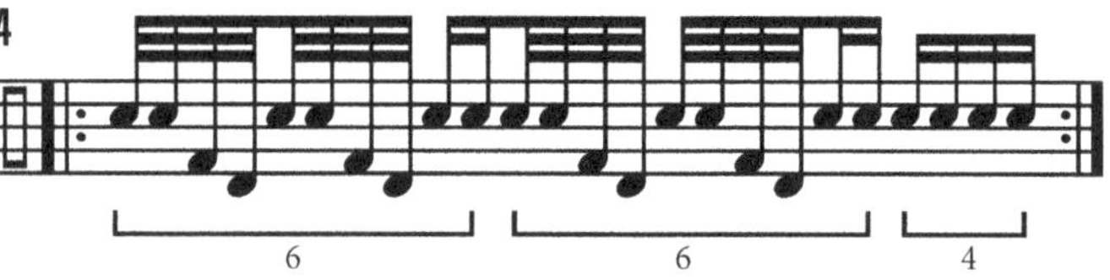

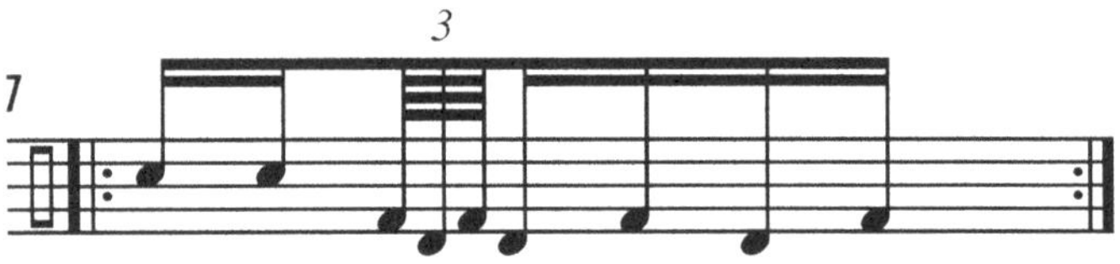

Seven-Note Linear Cross Rhythms

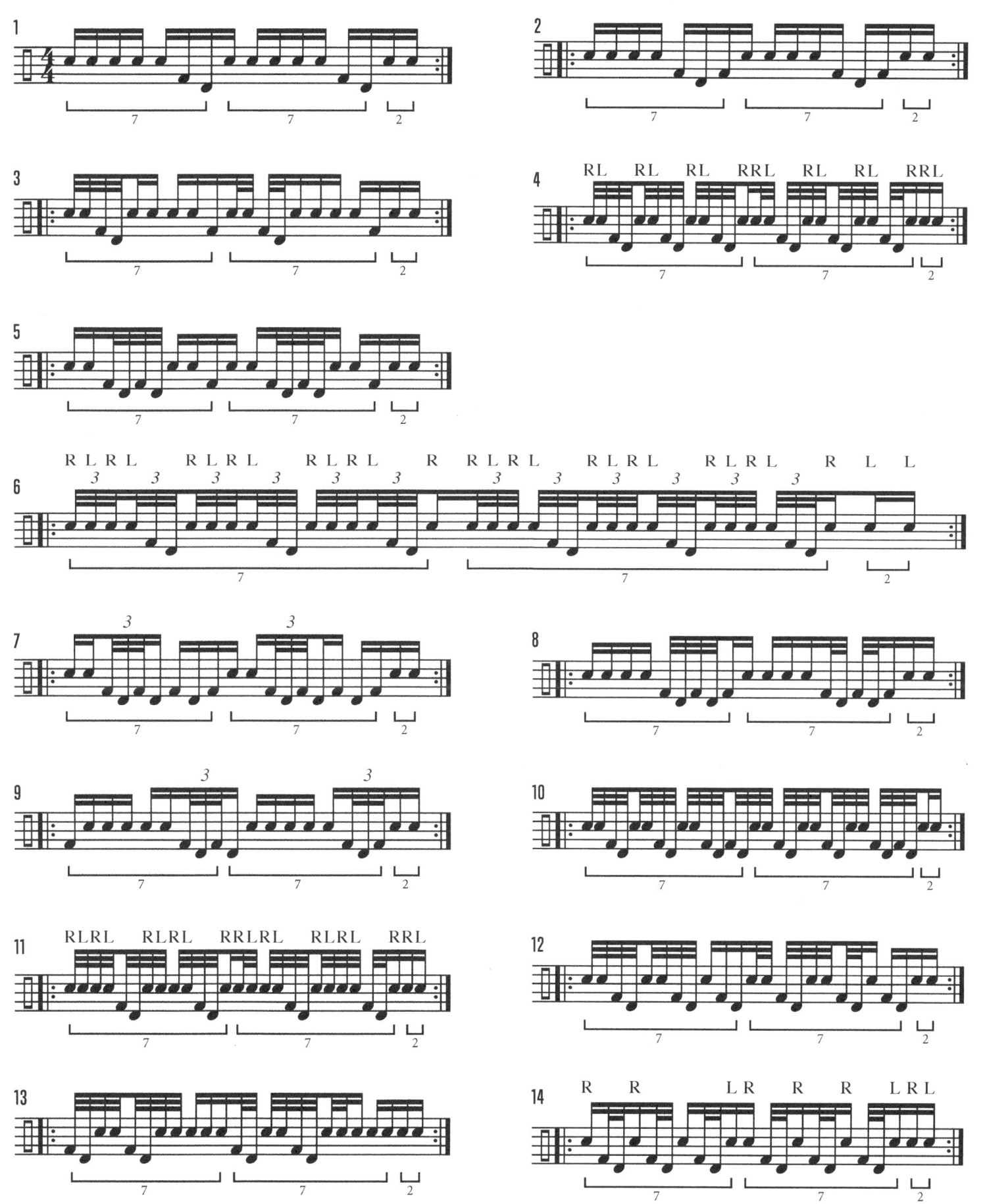

Encyclopedia Of Double Bass Drumming | 61

9/16 Grouping Warm-Ups

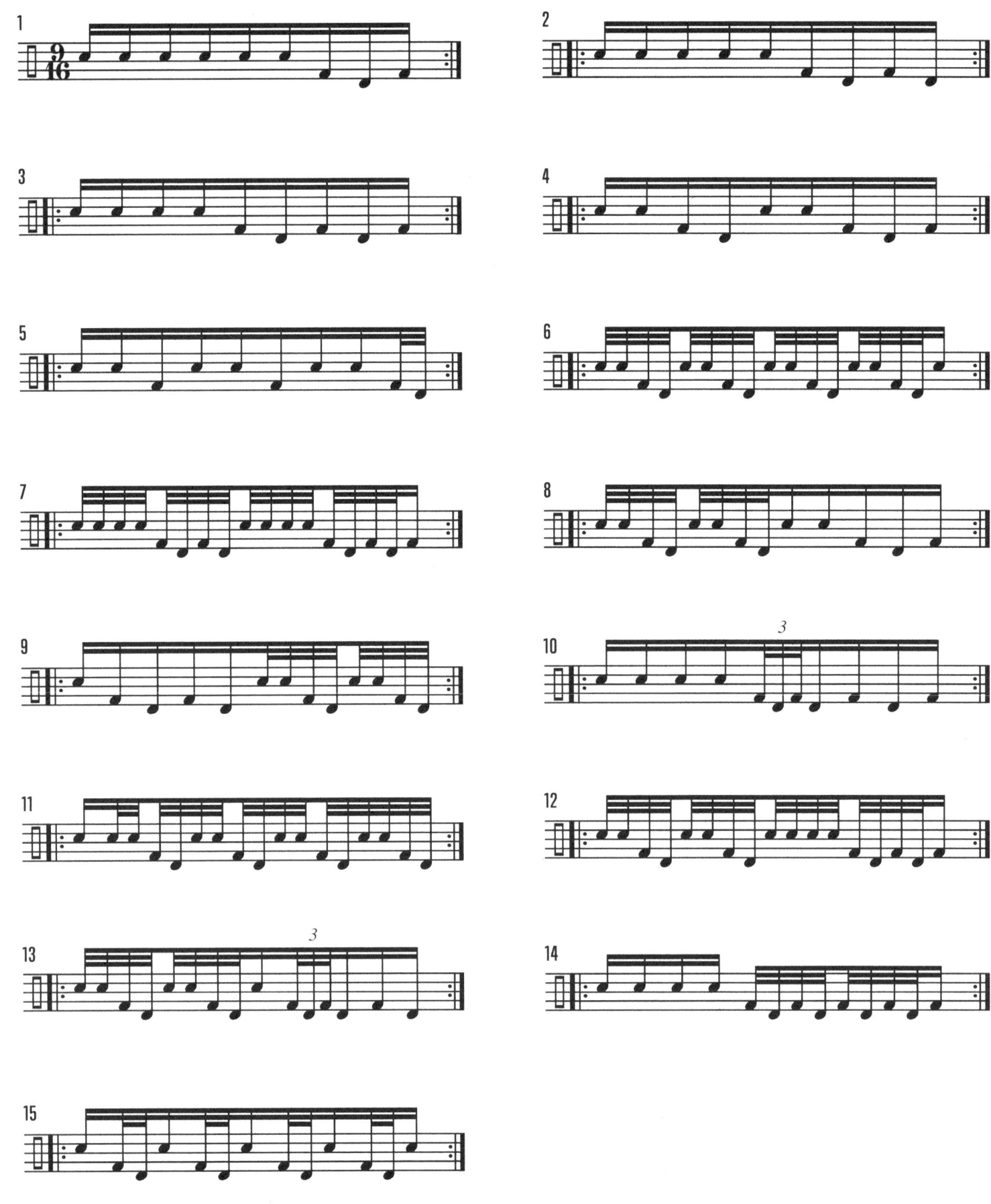

Encyclopedia Of Double Bass Drumming

Nine-Note Linear Cross-Rhythms

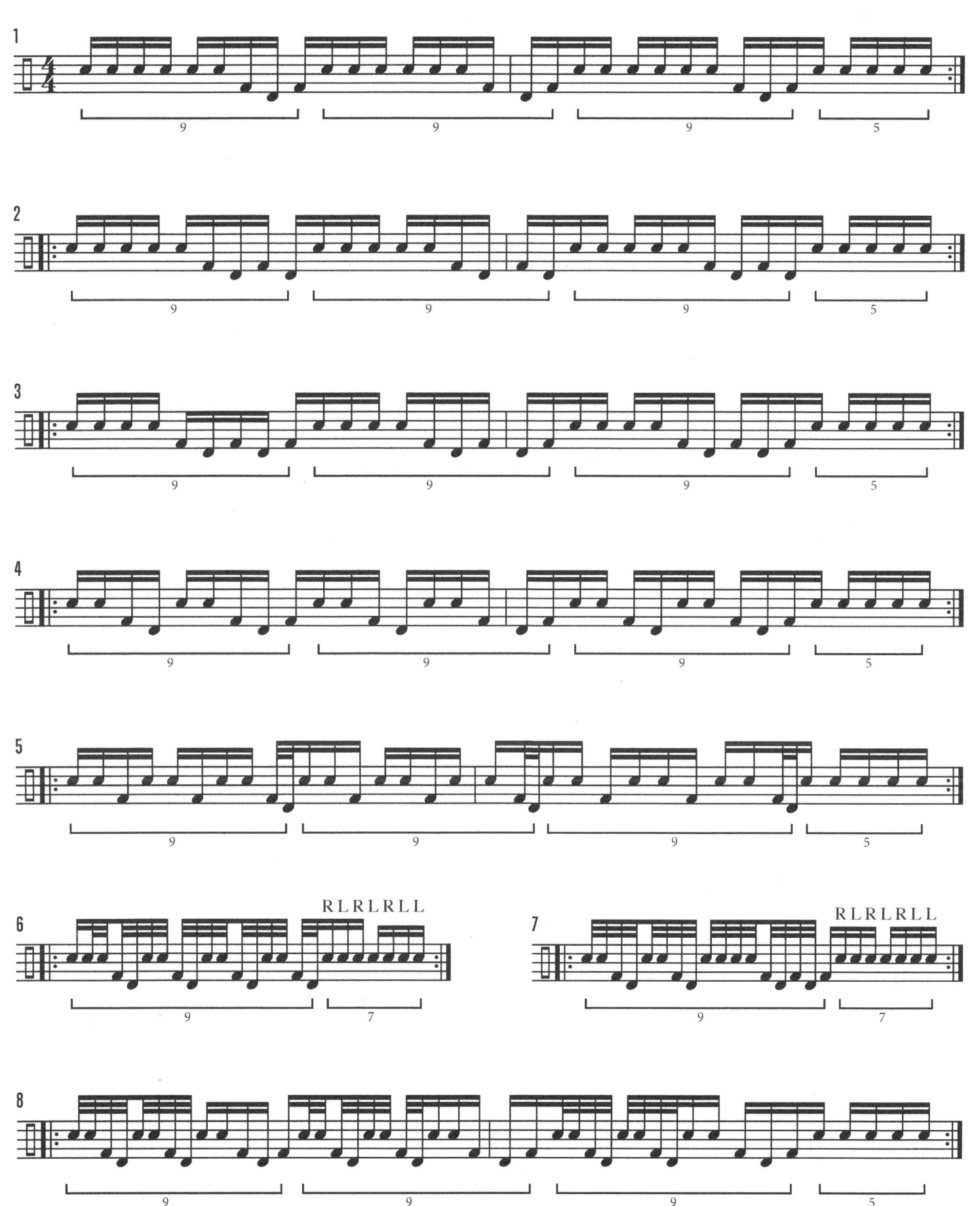

Encyclopedia Of Double Bass Drumming | 63

Four-Note-Triplet Linear Cross-Rhythms

9

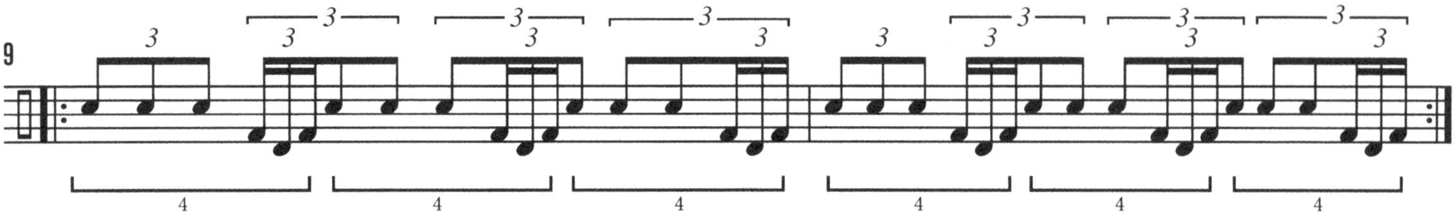

10

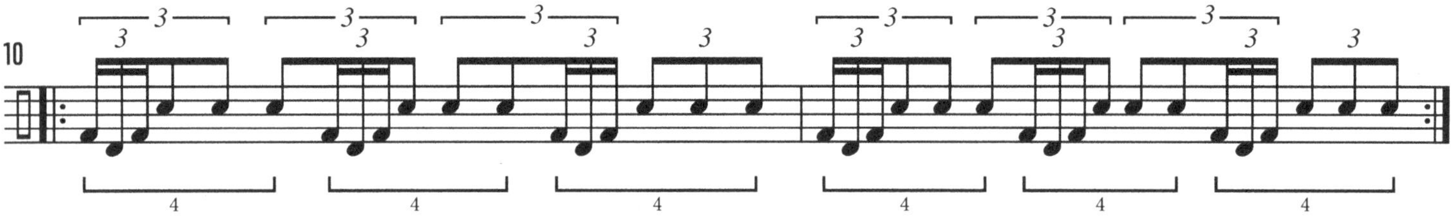

11

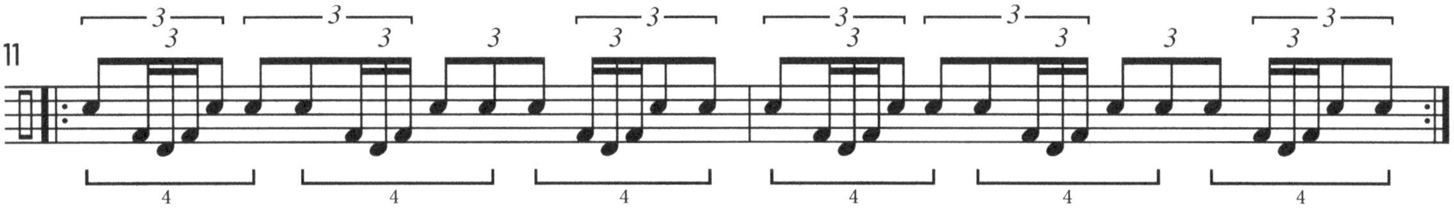

12

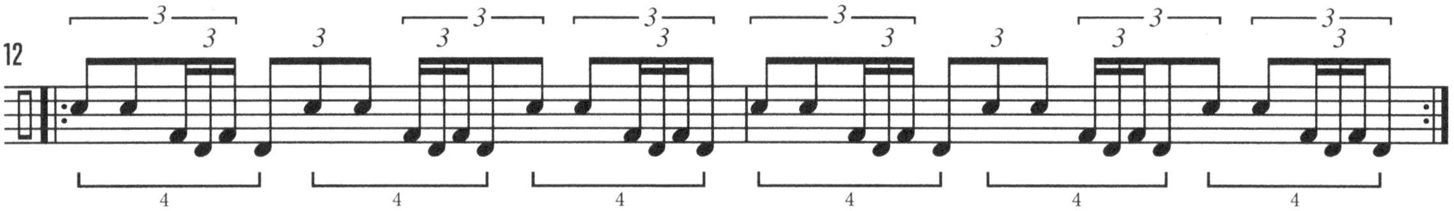

Five-Note-Triplet Linear Cross Rhythms

1

2

3

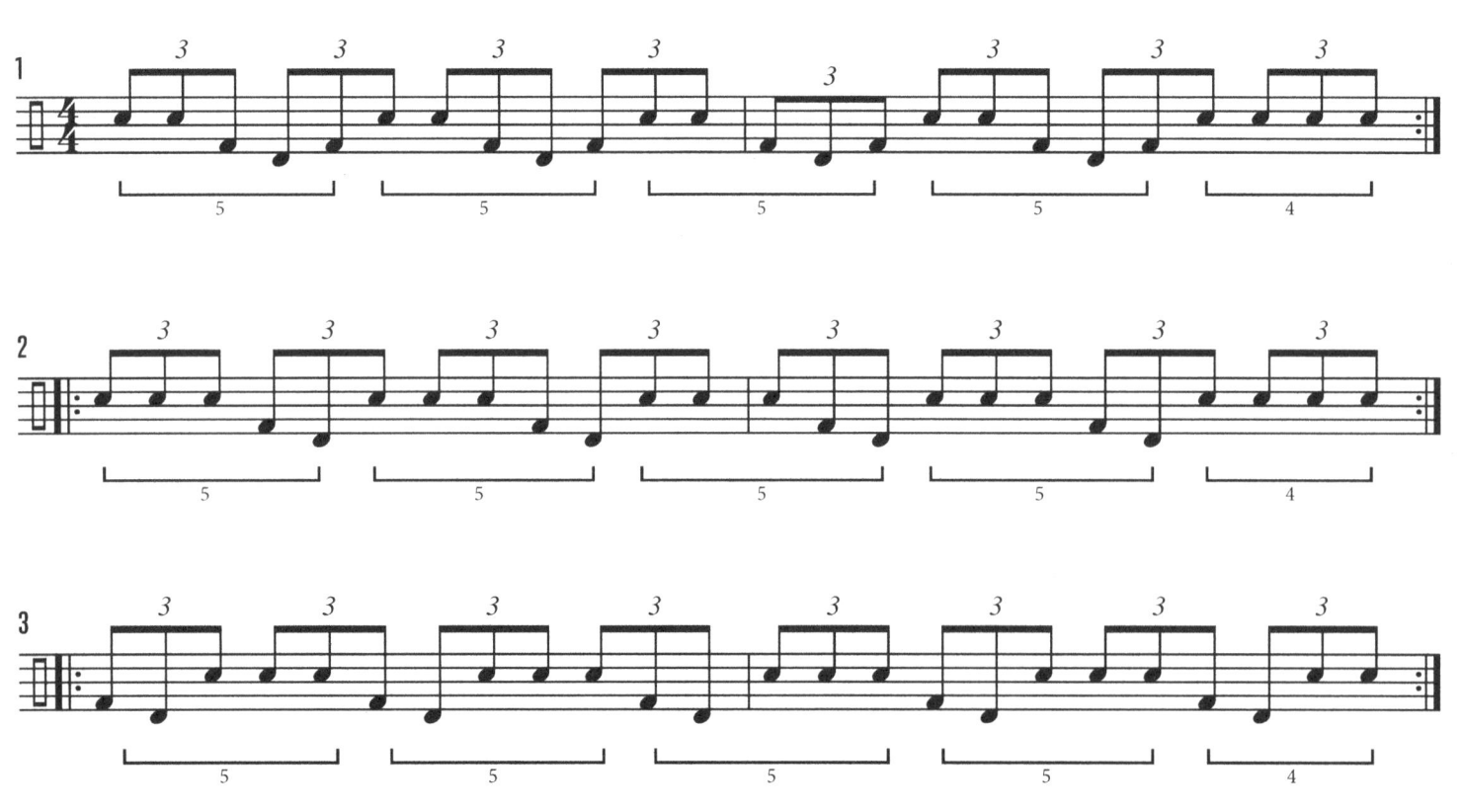

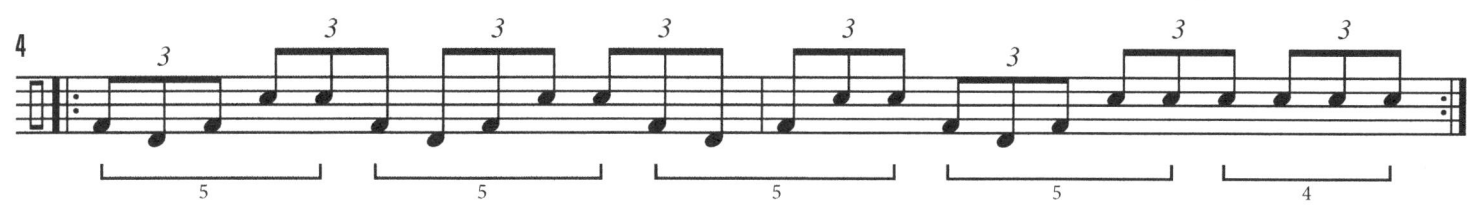
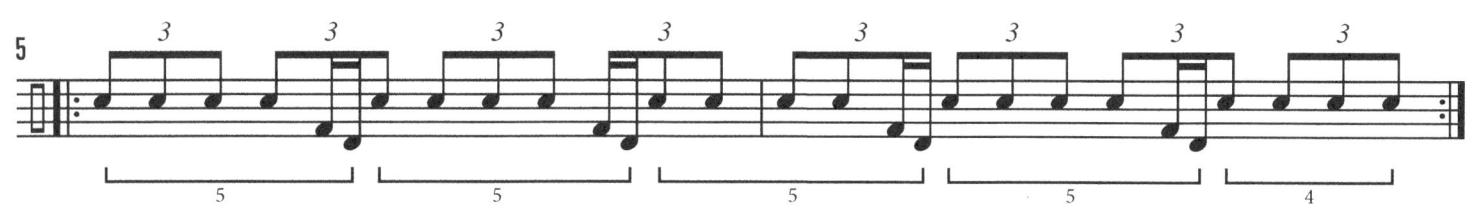

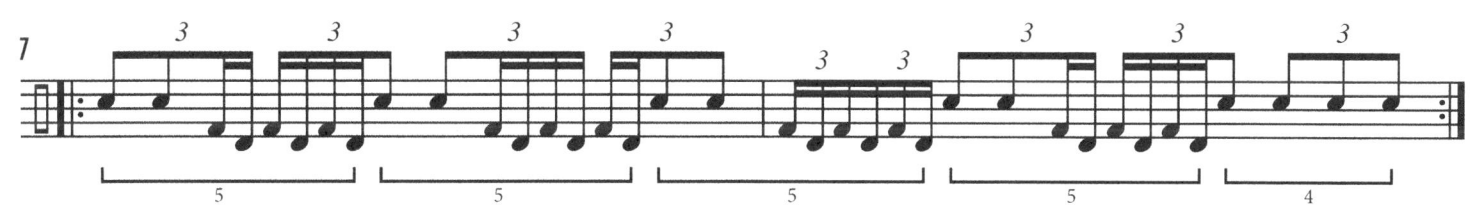
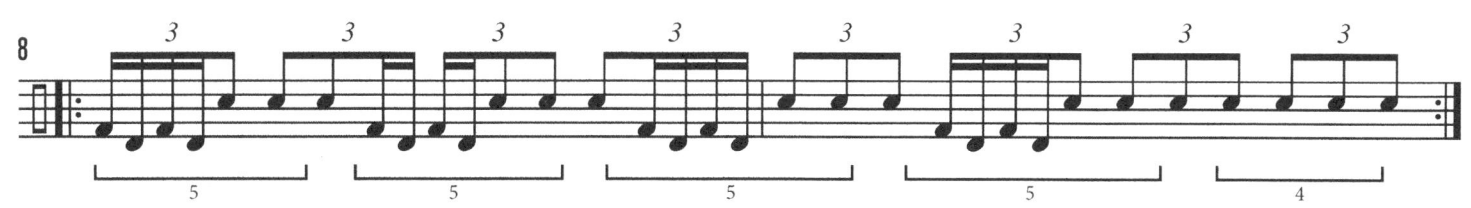
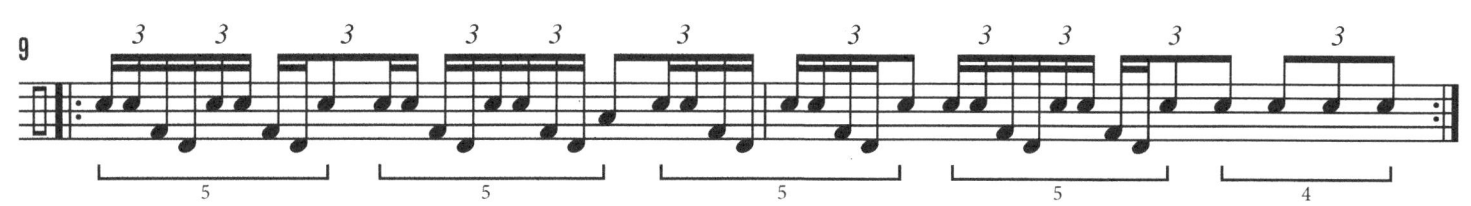

Encyclopedia Of Double Bass Drumming | 67

Seven-Note-Triplet Linear Cross-Rhythms

Chapter 13 Linear Cross-Rhythm Combinations

The following combinations will help you develop more linear cross-rhythm fills in addition to what's been presented so far. Any of the previously covered cross-rhythm *phrases* can be played using these combinations. However, the possibilities of cross-rhythm combinations are limitless. Experiment with your own combinations.

The groups of numbers below represent combinations of either 16th notes (in the 16th-note groupings) or 8th-note or 16th-note triplets (in the triplet groupings). Notice that these groupings of numbers add up to sixteen (for the 16th-note section) or twenty-four (two measures of 8th-note triplets or one measure of 16th-note triplets). Remember, the combination of numbers represents a cross-rhythm, and their order greatly affects the sound of the fill.

16th-Note Groupings In One-Bar Fills

A)	B)	C)	D)	E)
1. 33334	1. 5533	1. 772	1. 97	1. 943
2. 43333	2. 3355	2. 277	2. 79	2. 349
3. 34333	3. 3535	3. 727		3. 439
4. 33433	4. 5353			4. 934
5. 33343	5. 3553			5. 394
				6. 493

Triplet Groupings (Twenty-Four 8th-Note Triplets For Two Measures, Twenty-Four 16th-Note Triplets For One Measure)

A)	B)	C)	D)
1. 444444	1. 55554	1. 7773	1. 5577
	2. 45555	2. 3777	2. 5757
	3. 54555	3. 7377	3. 7575
	4. 55455	4. 7737	4. 5775
	5. 55545		5. 7557

Chapter 14 Fast Track Double Bass

- This chapter contains some of the most commonly played double bass licks.
- Just like any foundational technique, it's a good idea to have these exercises "under your feet" to be able to apply them at will.
- If you've methodically worked through the book at this point, these should not take you long to master.
- Both the Beats and Fills sections should be practiced at many tempos and with a metronome or drum machine.

Beats

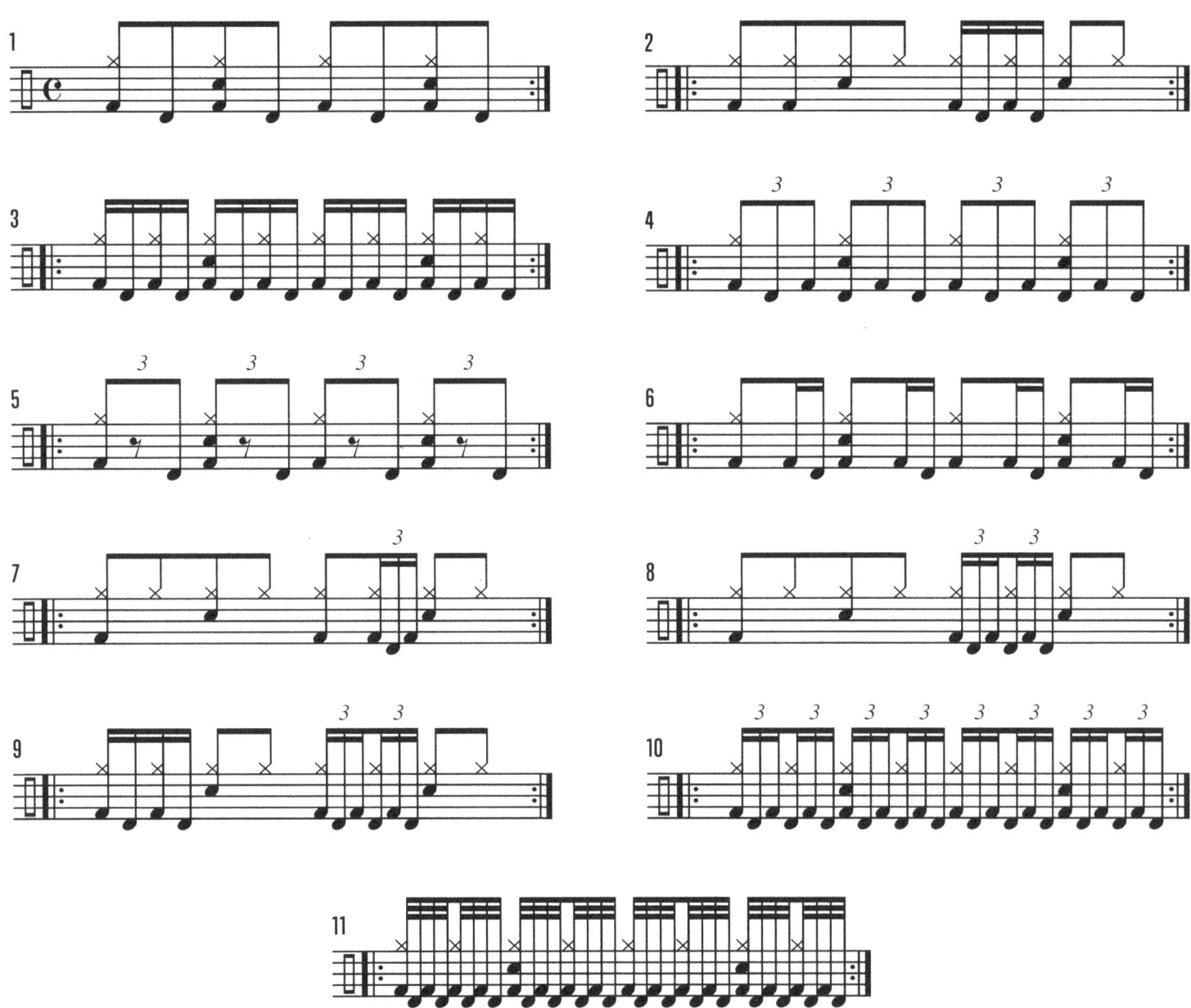

Fills

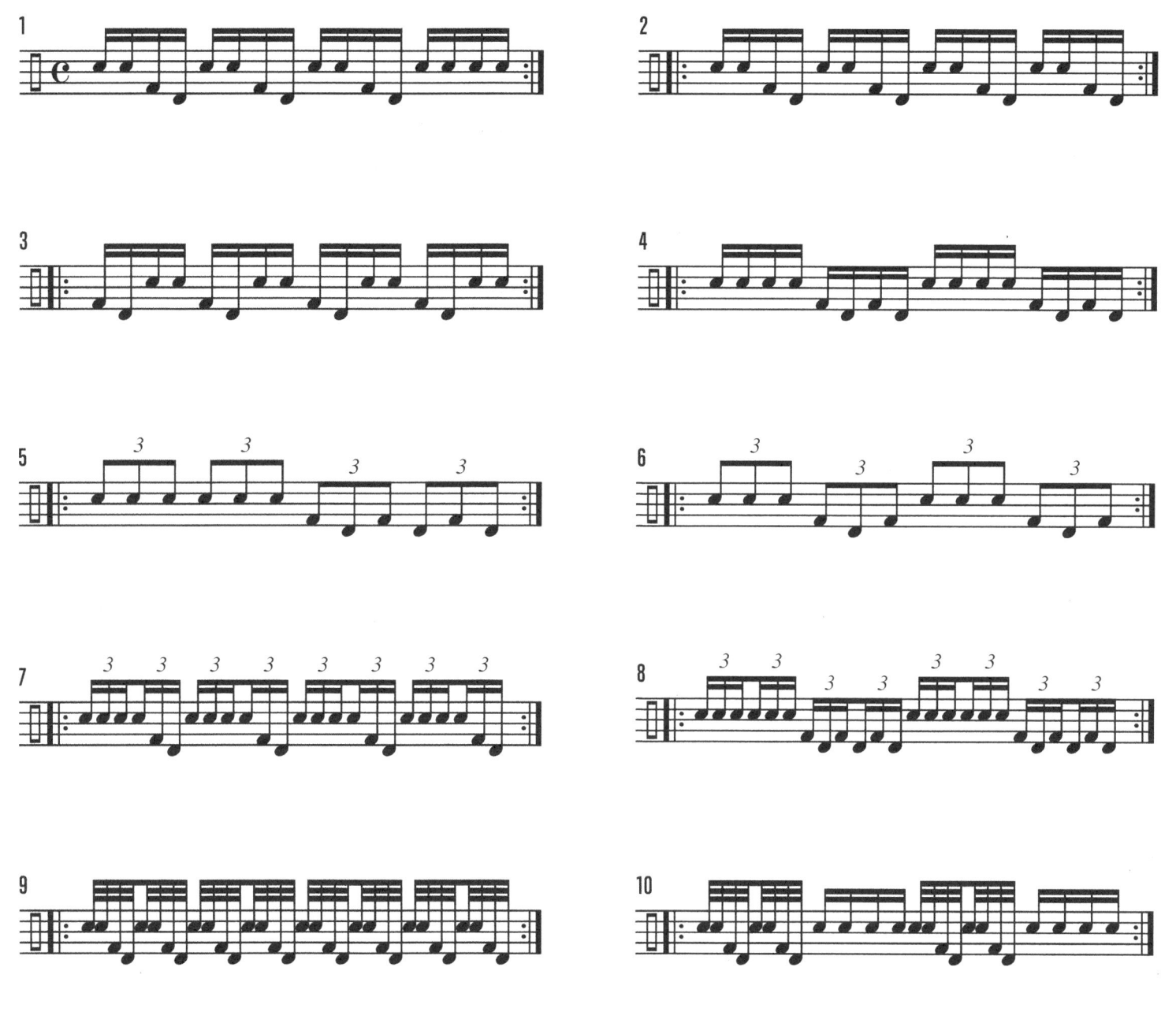

New Chapters by Bobby Rondinelli

This revised edition of the *Encyclopedia Of Double Bass Drumming* includes nine new chapters written by Bobby Rondinelli. This section covers contemporary techniques such as bass drum double strokes, feet-only exercises, binary and ternary rhythms, "skiplets", beat turnarounds, the "ladder", and playing doubles with the hands while playing singles with the feet.

These concepts will challenge your playing while expanding your double bass vocabulary. If practiced with intention and diligence, this material will help to prepare you for the demands of today's music.

This material is advanced, but completely attainable for anyone who has completed the previous chapters in this book. Always strive for great quality of sound and groove, and remember to start slowly at first. Have fun!

Chapter 15 Starters – Double Strokes

Playing double strokes with your feet is challenging, but well worth the time. Like everything else, it's difficult until it becomes easy.

If you are already playing double strokes with your feet, this section will show you some of the different combinations and footings. If you're not comfortable with playing doubles yet, stay on the first few exercises for a while. When you get them going, you can move on to the feet only section.

- Starters will get your feet going without worrying about your hands.
- This chapter will be most helpful for beginning double bass drummers when played at slow tempos.
- You can use the heel/toe method, toe/toe, or heel-down technique. Try them all to see what works best for you.
- Start slow. Practicing on a double bass practice pad can be very helpful—tapping your feet on the floor is practicing!
- Work with a metronome.

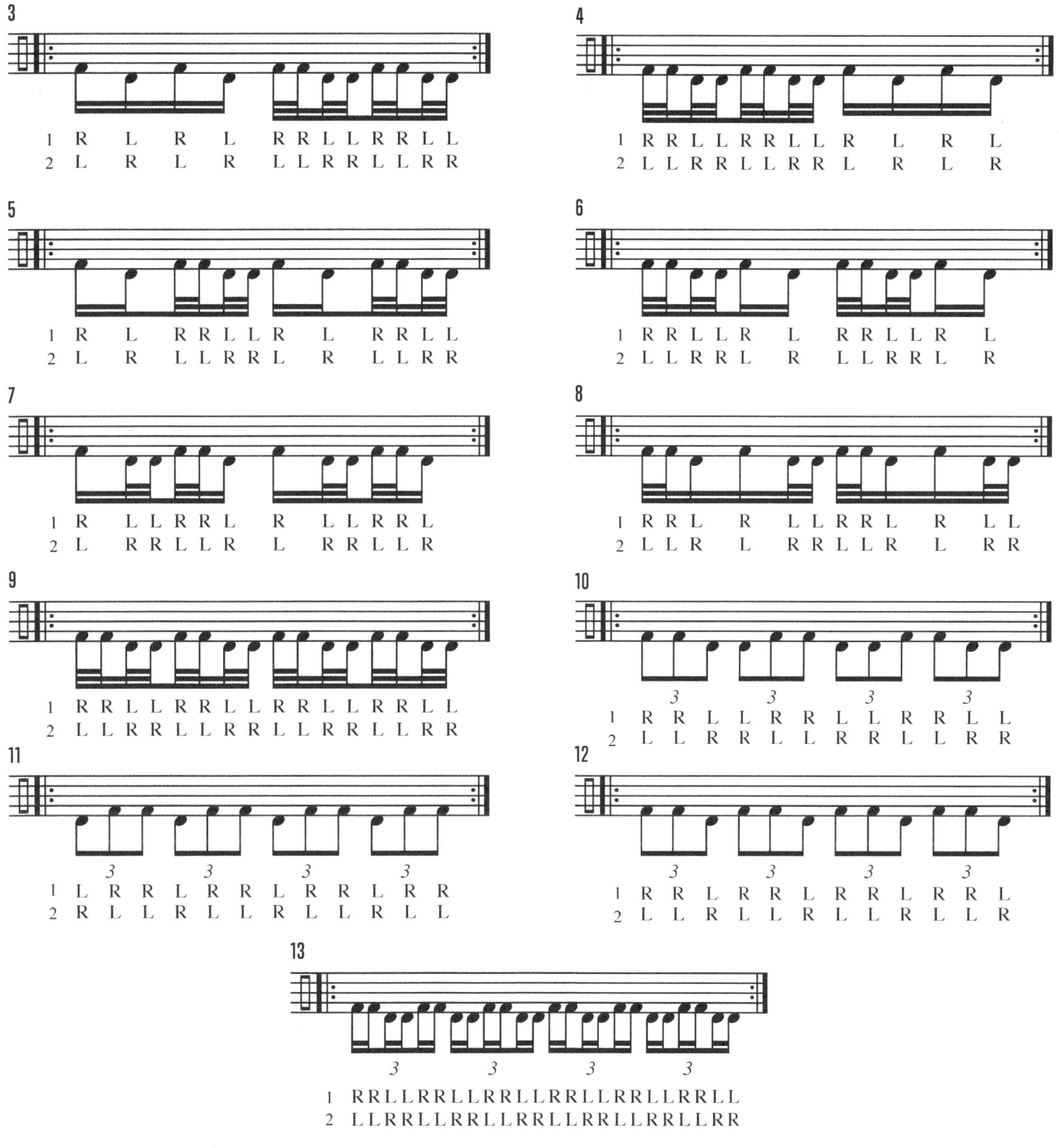

Chapter 16 Feet Only

The "Feet Only" chapter is designed to help you drop in 32nd-note doubles within a 16th-note single-bass groove. Double strokes are usually lower in volume than single strokes, so be sure to play them with power. Don't worry about speed, I always say "worrying about speed will slow you down!"

- Start slowly.
- Remember that the rhythm is more important than the written footing—my right foot might be your left.
- The exercises get more difficult as the chapter goes on. Stay relaxed and focused.
- Work with a metronome.

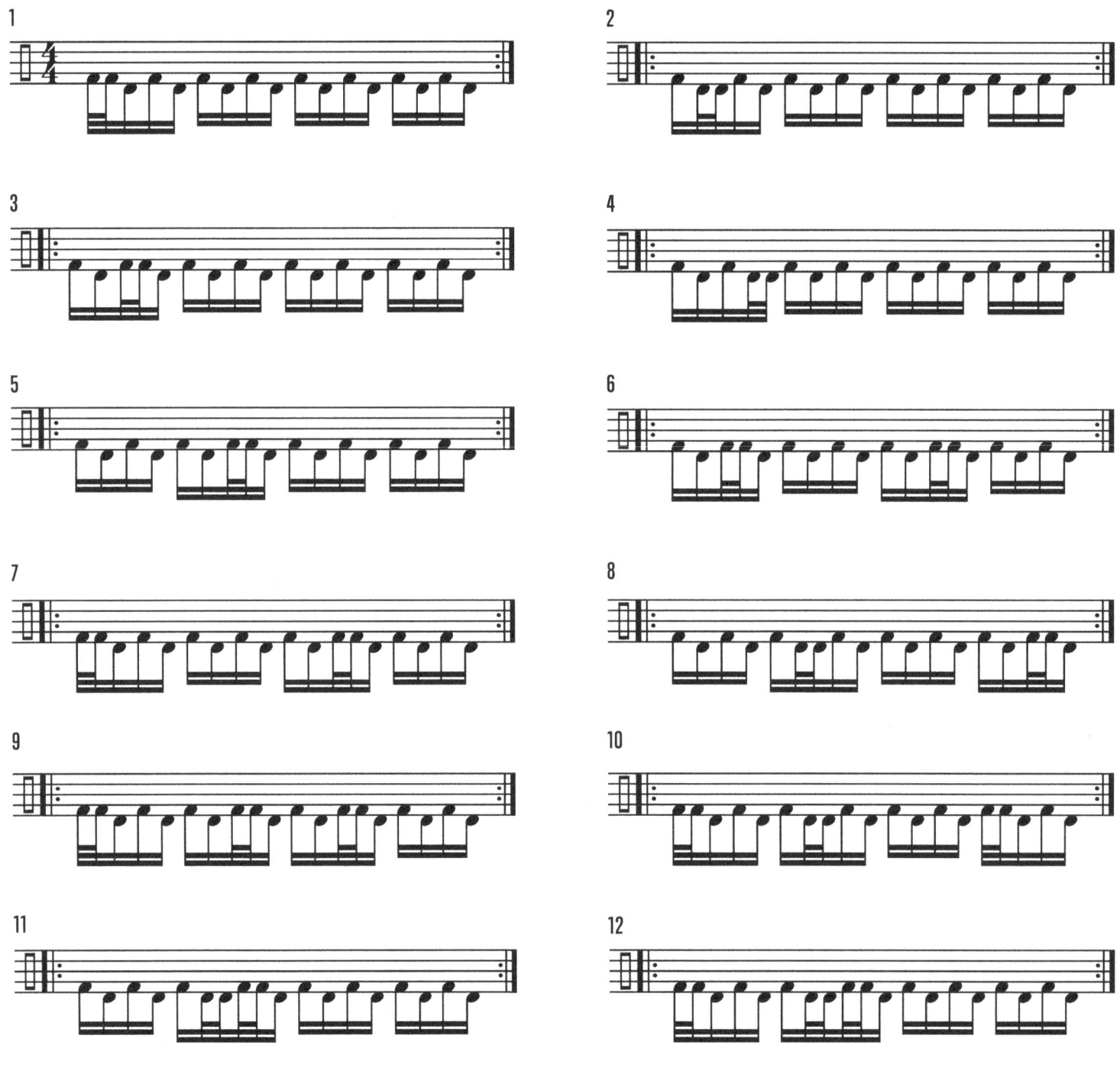

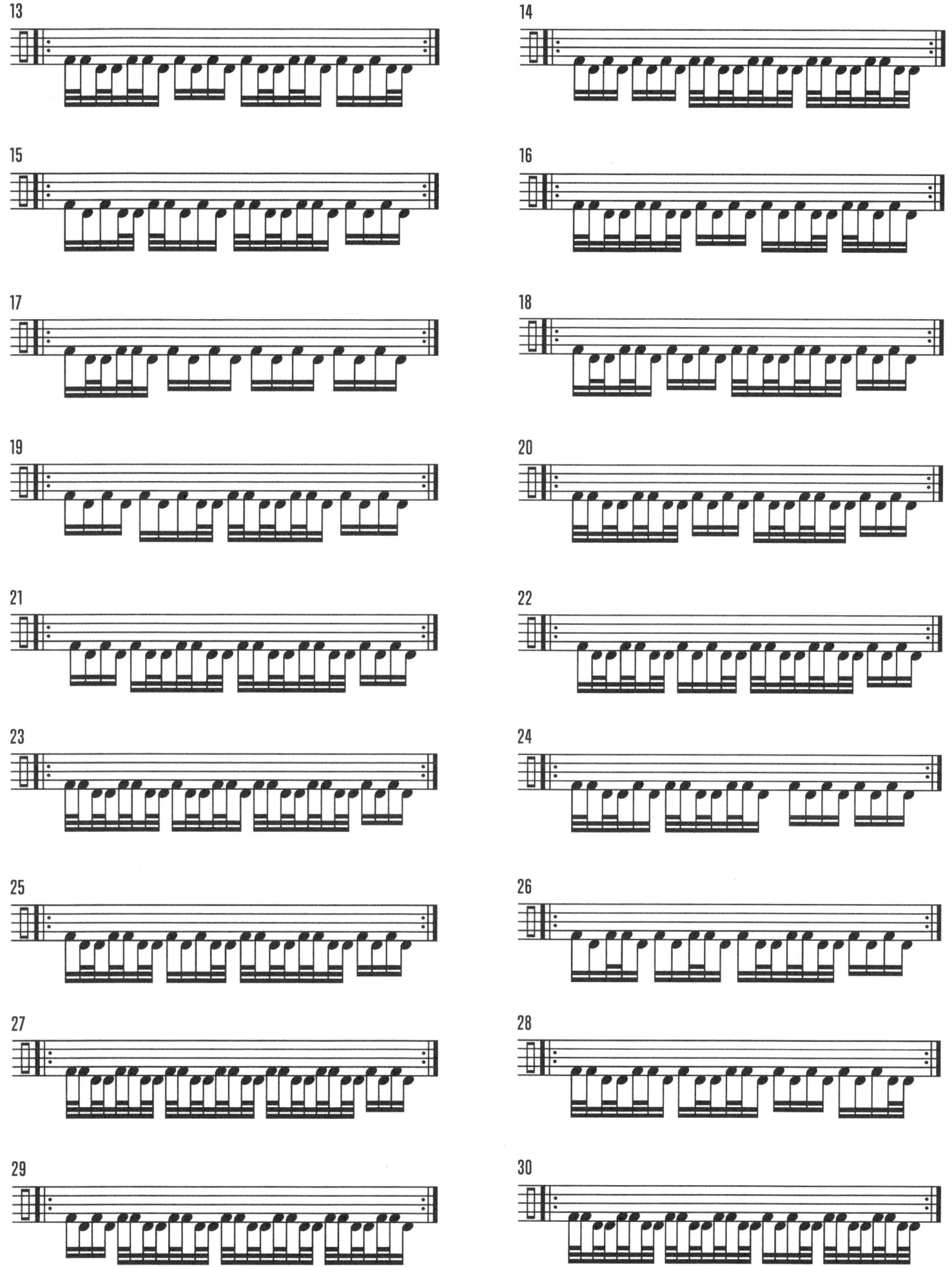

Chapter 17 Binary Beats and Fills

This section contains 1-bar, 2-bar, and 4-bar beats—some with fills. There is also a section dedicated to fills only. Remember that most beats are written with strong foot-lead (If you are right-handed, then that would be your right foot.) Some right-handed players lead with their left foot—whatever works for you is ok.

- Don't flam the snare, make sure it lands right on the bass drum.
- In the beginning, lighten up on your snare hit so that you can really hear where it is hitting in relation to the bass drum.
- Don't worry about speed—try to make your feet sound even.
- Work on getting your weak foot to sound as loud as your strong foot.

Beats

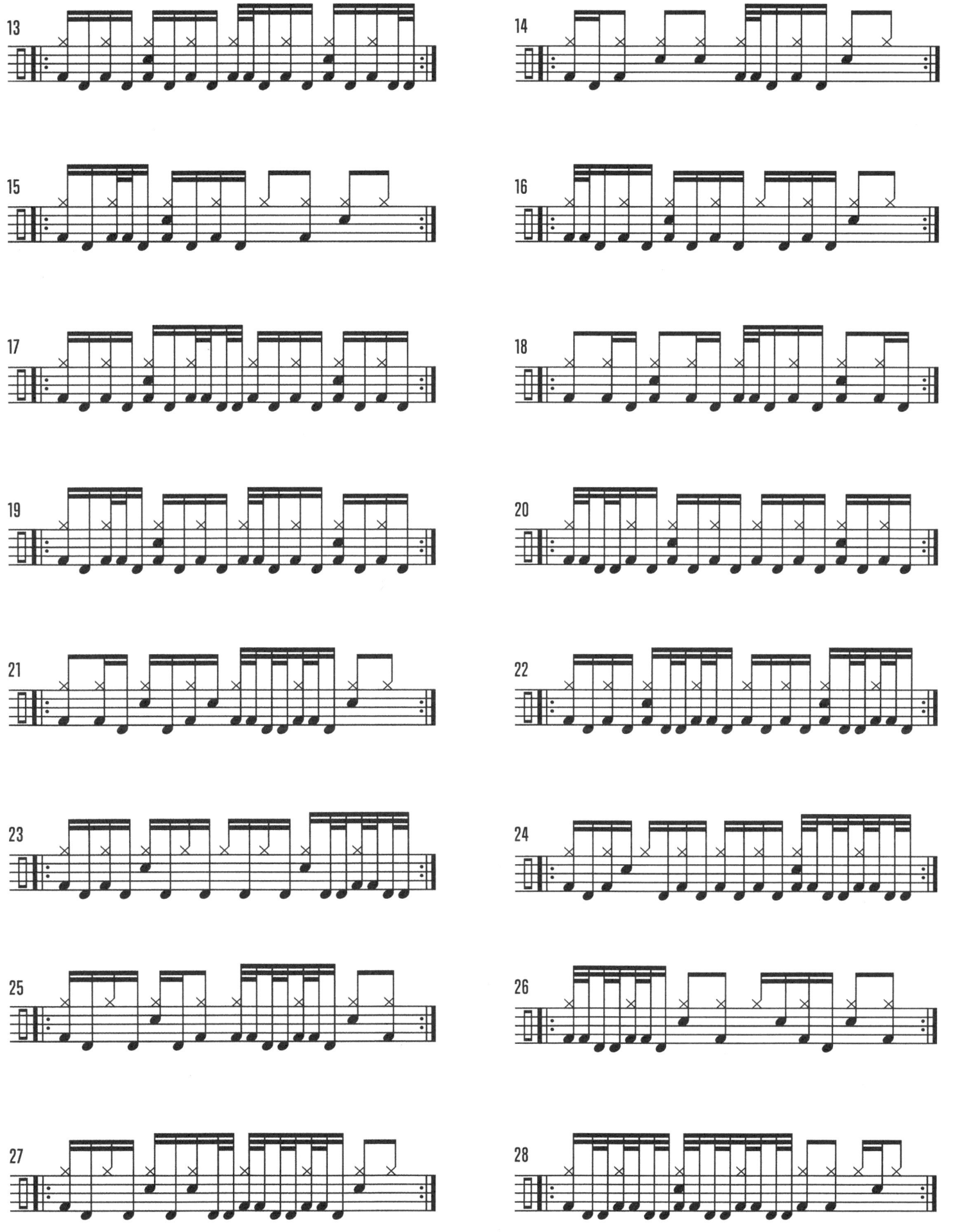

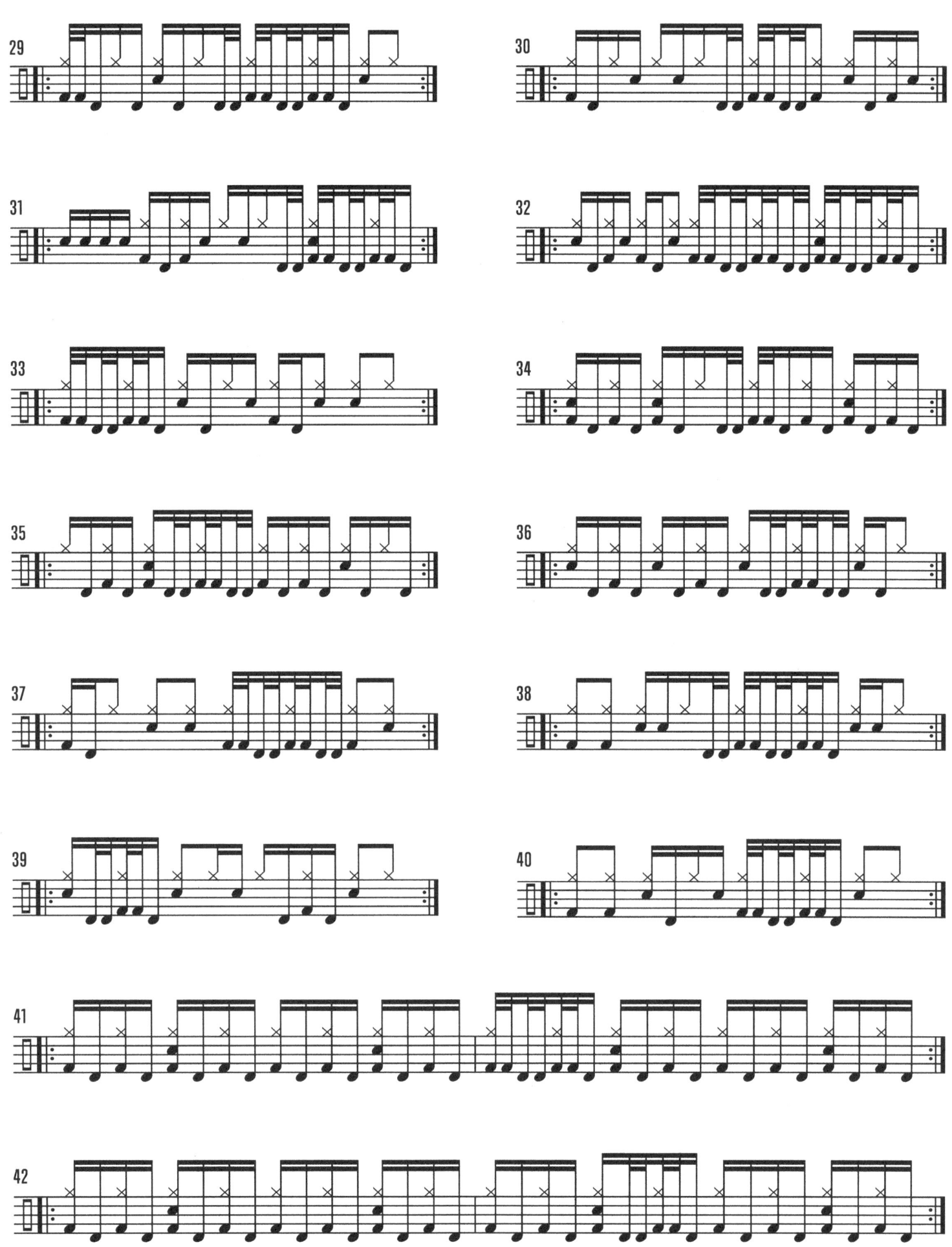

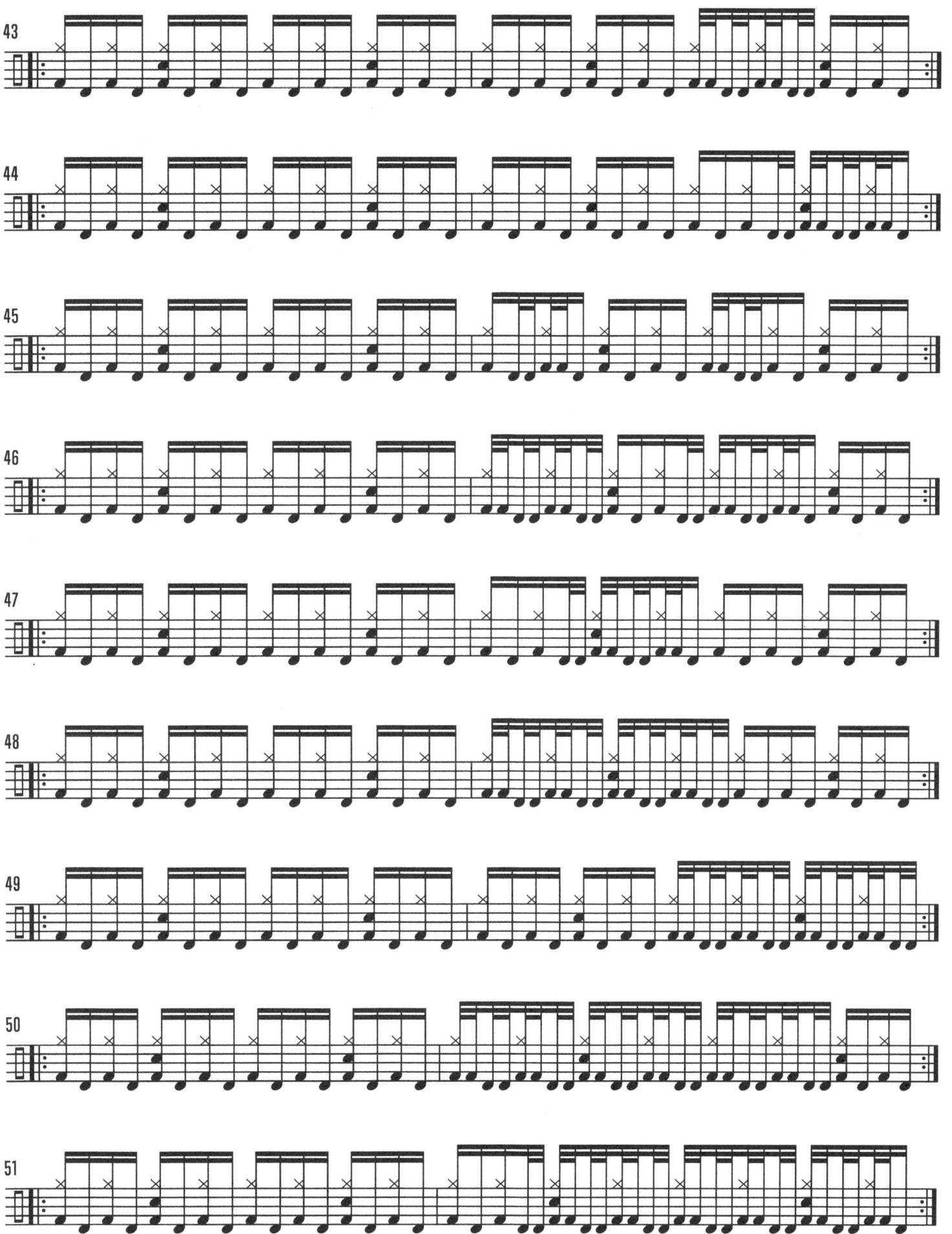

Fills

82 | Encyclopedia Of Double Bass Drumming

Chapter 18: Feet Only – Triplets

In this section, you will be dropping 16th-note triplet doubles into an 8th-note triplet pattern.

- Remember your balance, stay centered.
- Posture is very important—don't lean forward or backwards.
- Start slowly and work your way up.

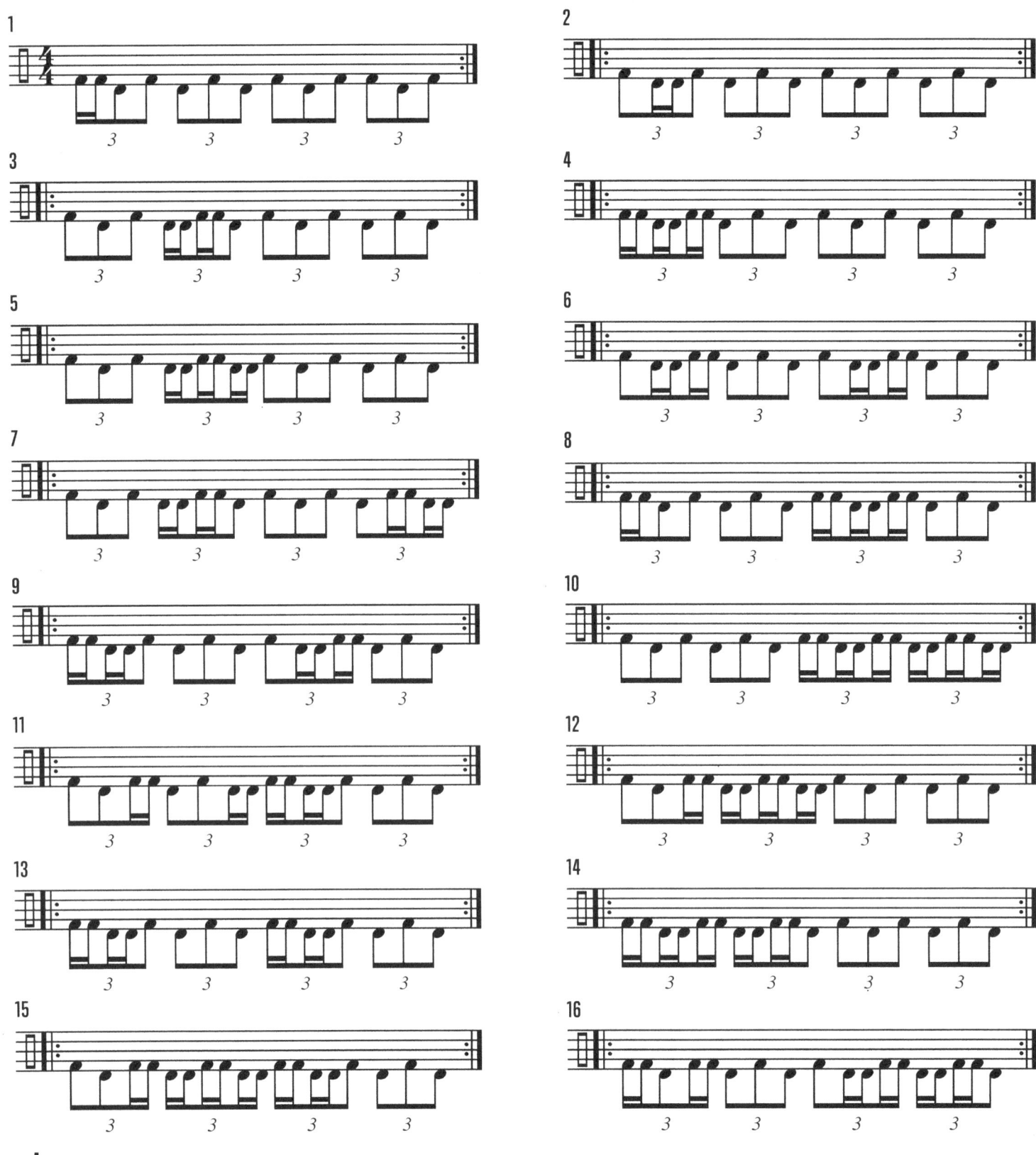

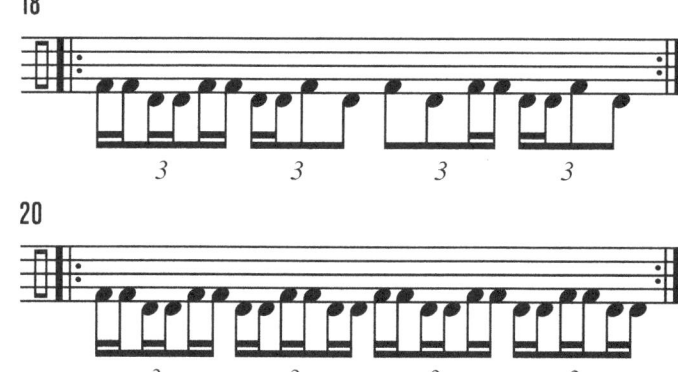

Chapter 19 Ternary Beats and Fills

This section has triplet beats and fills of different lengths—1 to 4 bars. Some are continuous triplets, and some are broken up.

- Stay relaxed and focused.
- Feel free to move around to different examples. If a beat is too difficult, you can always go back to it.

Beats

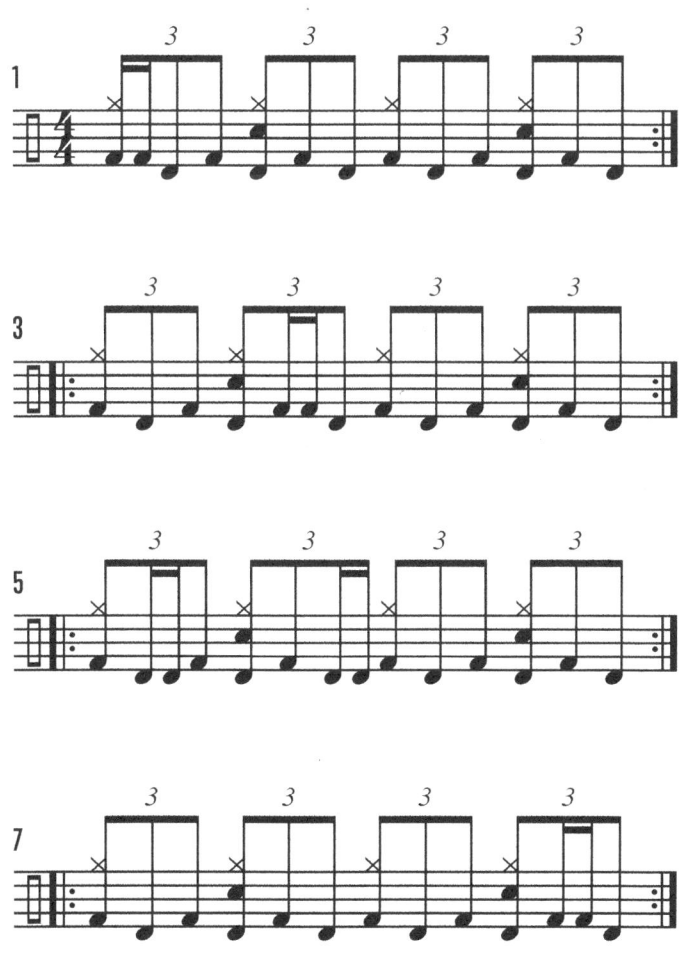
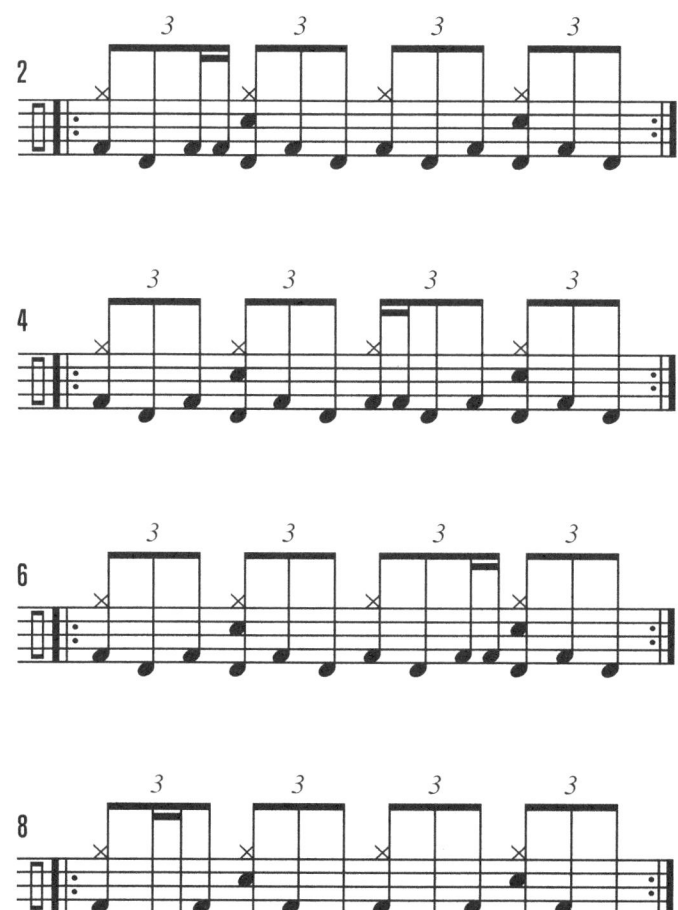

Encyclopedia Of Double Bass Drumming

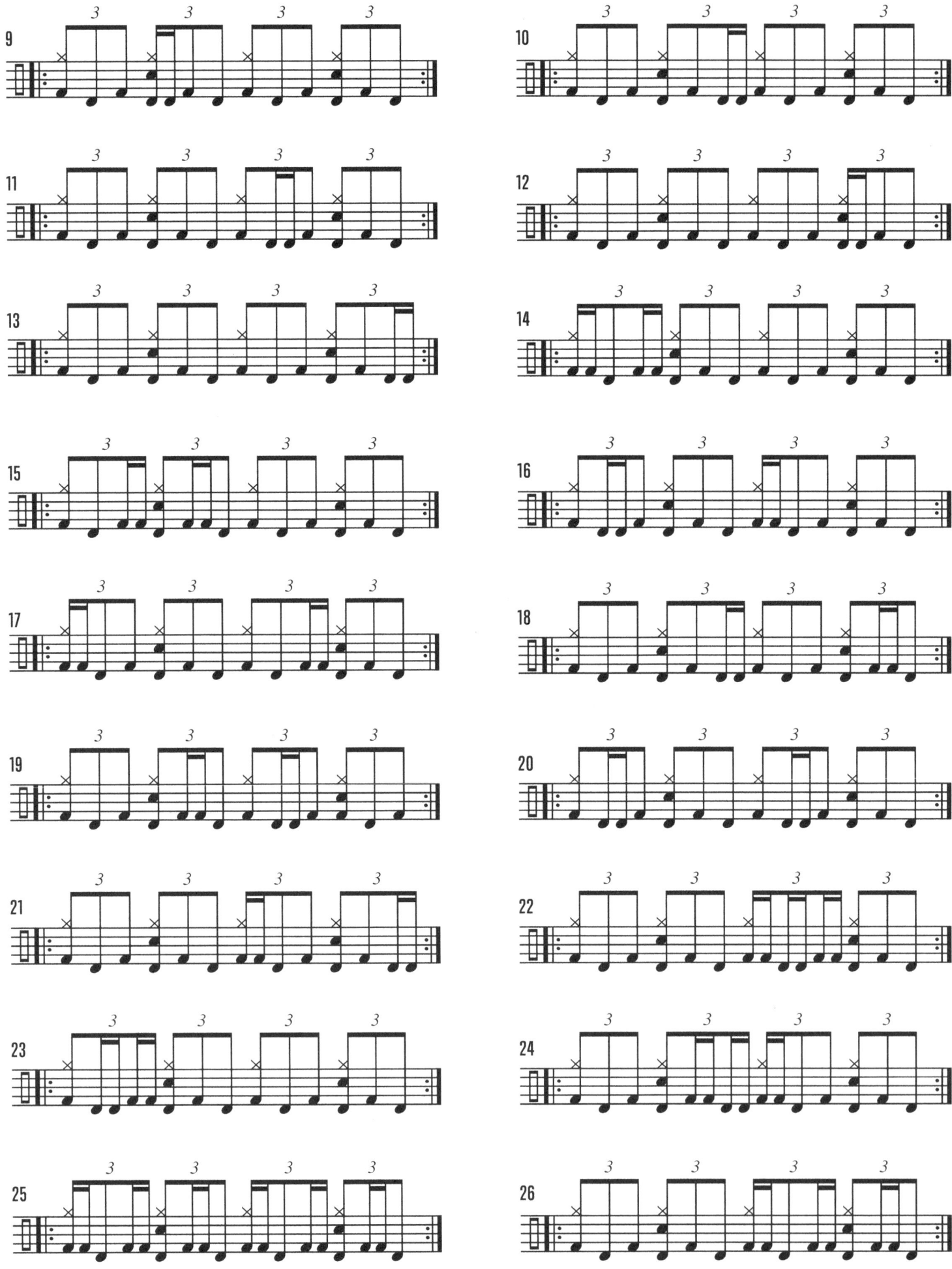

Fills

Encyclopedia Of Double Bass Drumming | 91

Chapter 20 Skiplets

Skiplets are triplets where one foot plays the first triplet partial, and the other foot plays the next two. They can be in any combination—try starting or ending with one.

- Try all the possible footings in the warm-ups.
- You will find which skiplets suit your style.
- The beats and fills have many skiplet patterns. Feel free to substitute the ones that you like best.
- Skiplets can also be played with the left foot on the hi-hat and left bass drum pedal together.

Warm-Ups

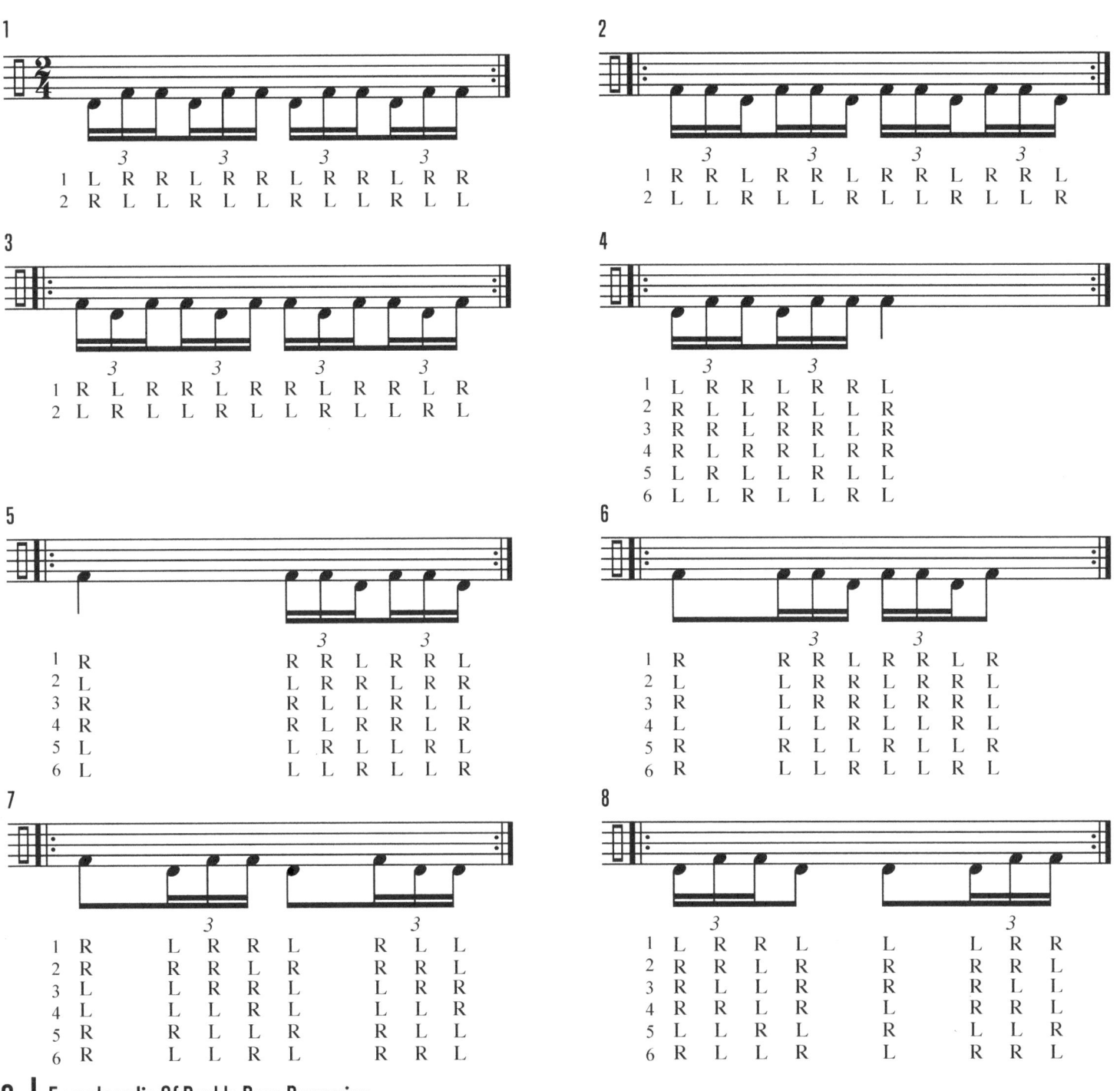

92 | Encyclopedia Of Double Bass Drumming

Beats

• Left foot can be played as bass drum or bass drum and hi-hat together.

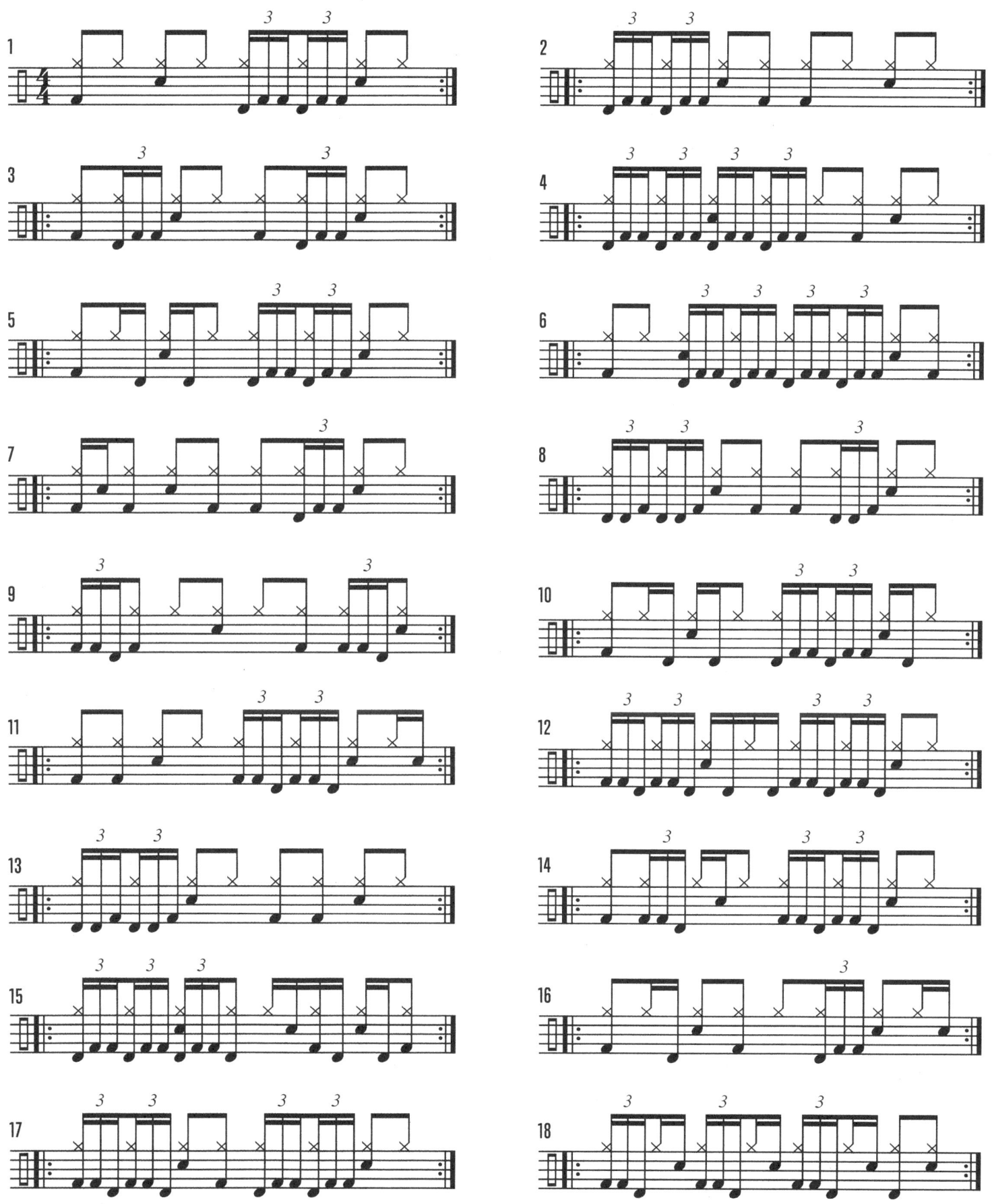

94 | Encyclopedia Of Double Bass Drumming

Fills

Encyclopedia Of Double Bass Drumming | 95

Chapter 21: Turn the Beat Around (Turnarounds)

"Turning the beat around" is when you play a double-bass pattern that changes your downbeat foot to an upbeat, and your upbeat foot to a downbeat. This chapter contains many warm-ups, beats and fills that will help you develop this concept.

- Turnarounds are very powerful.
- Start slowly.
- Practice on and off of the pedals—tap your feet on the floor.
- Balance is very important.

Feet Only Warm-Ups

Beats

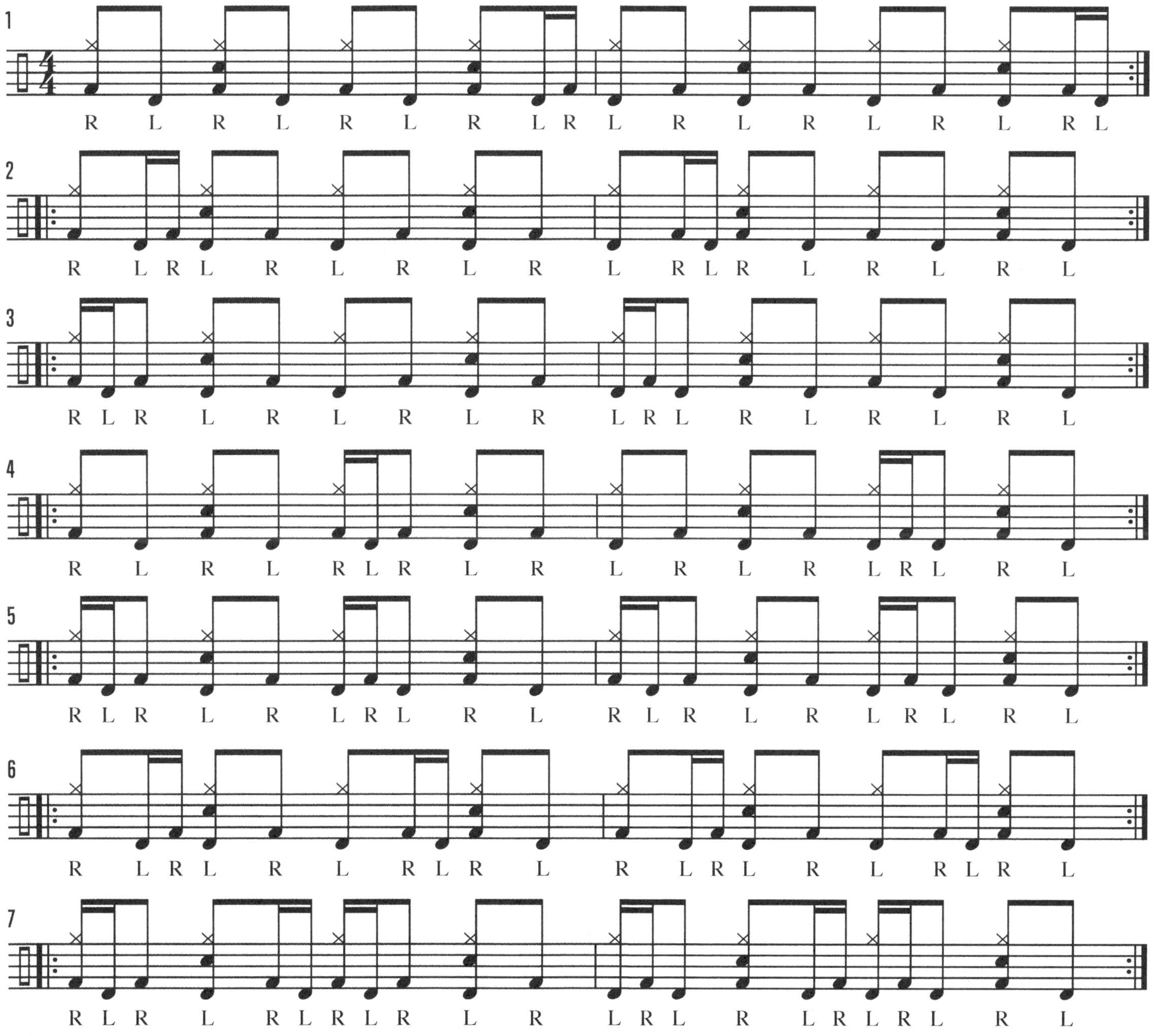

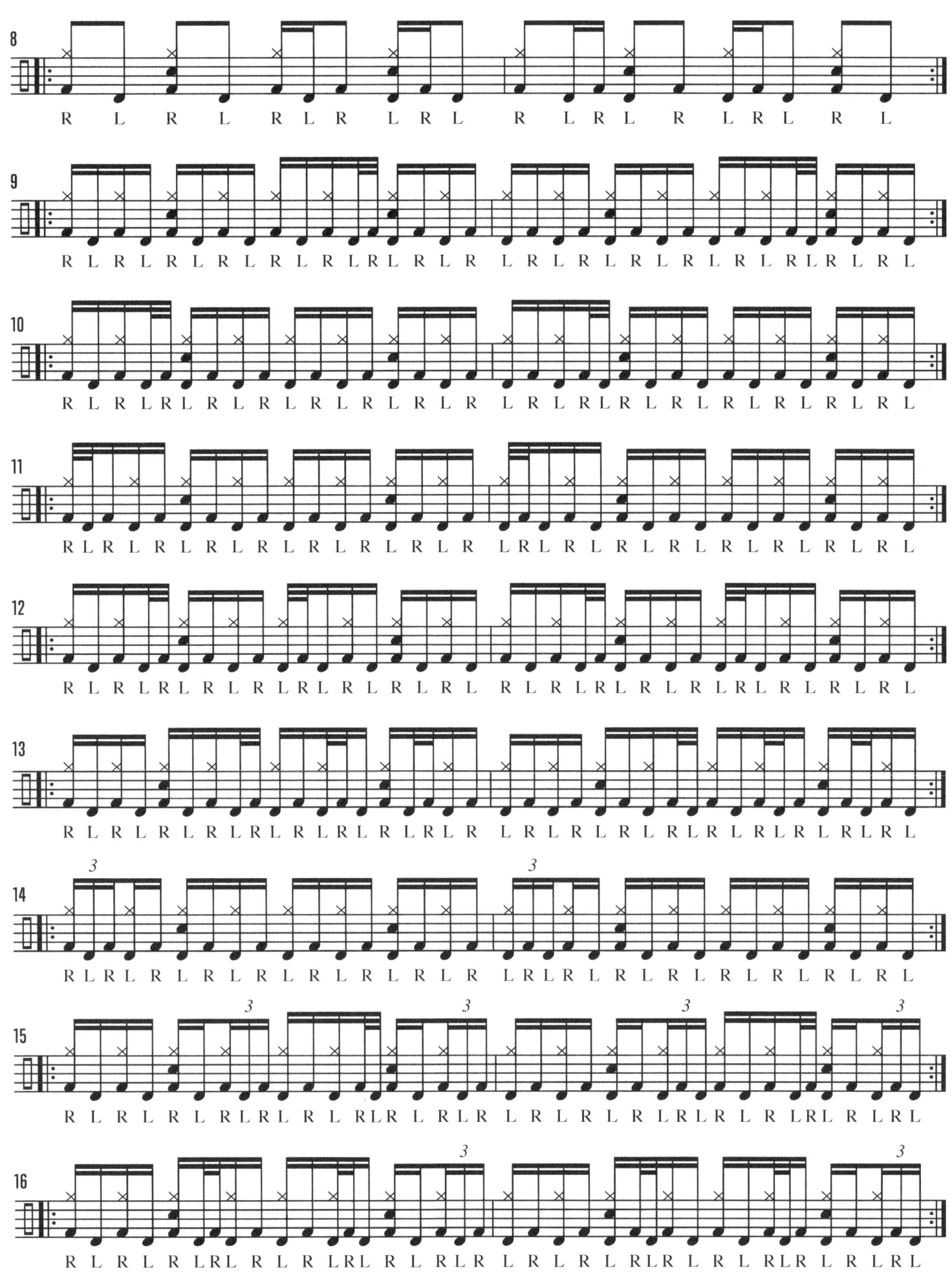

Chapter 22: The Ladder

This chapter originally appeared in the September 2007 issue of *Modern Drummer* magazine. The text that follows has been preserved from that article.

A few months ago I got together with *Modern Drummer* editor-in-chief Bill Miller to play some of the new chapters I was developing for a new edition of my book, *The Encyclopedia of Double Bass Drumming*. We spent a fun afternoon playing through patterns and exchanging ideas.

At one point Bill asked me if I'd ever played this hand-foot combination: right hand, left foot, left hand, right foot. He mentioned it was something that he worked on and loved the sound of. Apparently drummers like Vinnie Colaiuta and Gregg Bissonette have mastered this combo and do amazing things with it. Well, I told Bill I hadn't played it but that I'd work on it. A few days later, I called him to say how much fun I was having with it and how working on this pattern was like climbing a ladder.

I feel that the ladder is one of the newest and most unusual-sounding double bass patterns to come along in a while. Of course, anybody who plays double bass has played quads: right hand, left hand, right foot, left foot.

Since the 1960s, quads have been king. But the ladder is the future. Again, it's simply right hand, left foot, left hand, right foot. While it looks somewhat similar to quads on the page, it's completely different-sounding.

The ladder is much more difficult to play than quads, because the hands are playing singles while the feet are playing singles in-between the hands. But the sound of the ladder is very "centered" and much more powerful.

Bill explained to me that the best way to begin developing a feel for the ladder is to think in triplets. (He mentioned that's how he heard Bissonette explain it.) Try playing the next example very slowly. Don't increase the speed until you really begin to feel the "motion" of the pattern. (Once you have this down, you'll be able to move to the rest of the examples a lot easier.)

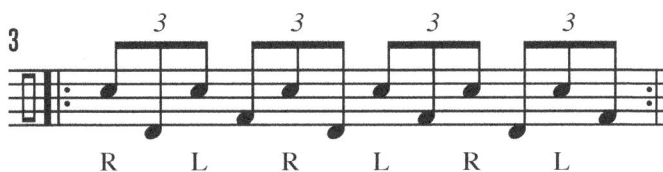

For the next example, which is in 16th notes instead of triplets, your hands stay constant while your feet move in and out of the pattern.

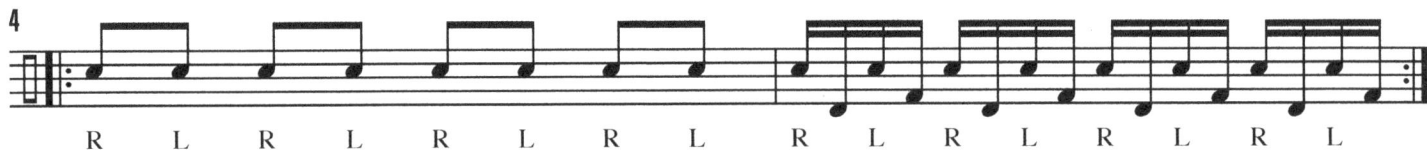

Let's take that same approach, but apply it to triplets.

Once you have the previous examples together, you can take the ladder in many different directions. I've been experimenting with patterns in which the feet stay constant and the hands drop in and out. So essentially I'm inverting the ladder so it will start with a foot, this way the feet don't have to change their motion.

In Example 6, start by slowly playing the 8th-note double bass pattern (in the first measure), and then drop in the hands between the feet in the second measure. Again, start this *very* slowly.

Now try playing a 16th–note pattern. Be sure to keep the ladder even; don't "flam" the sound.

The last example involves a triplet groove that moves into a ladder fill.

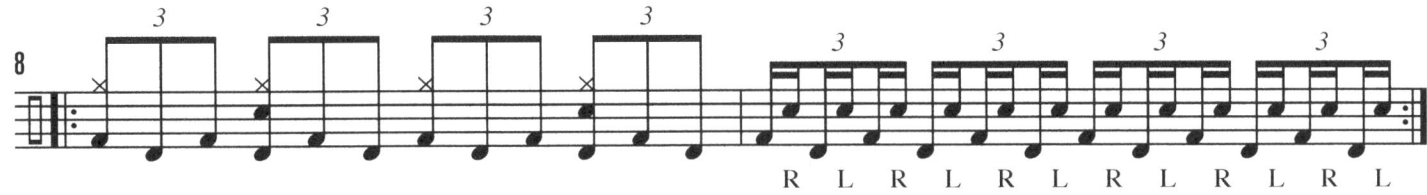

Take your time with these ideas and be sure to start out at a very slow tempo. Like everything else, it's hard until it becomes easy. But once you get it, you'll see how cool the ladder sounds. Enjoy!

Chapter 23: Double-Stroke Hands, Single-Stroke Feet

This chapter originally appeared in the January 2007 issue of *Modern Drummer* magazine. The text that follows has been preserved from that article.

Getting used to playing doubles with your hands while your feet are playing singles can be quite challenging. But it's worth the time invested. I use doubles with the hands because most people can play a double-stroke roll more evenly, and for longer periods of time than they can play singles. The feet are also good followers. If you play a rhythm with your hands, then you can follow along with your feet. Start the rolls with the right hand and right foot first, and then alternate the stickings.

Example 2 has a five-stroke roll in the hands with a five-stroke ruff in the feet. This exercise will help you gain control in short spurts, while also leaching you to lead with either foot. Start slowly. Accuracy is more important than speed

In Example 3, we have a nine-stroke roll in the hands and a nine-stroke ruff in the feet. When it starts to lock in, increase the speed.

Example 4 is an open roll in the hands with the feet playing singles. Try this one (as well as the other exercises) at different tempos.

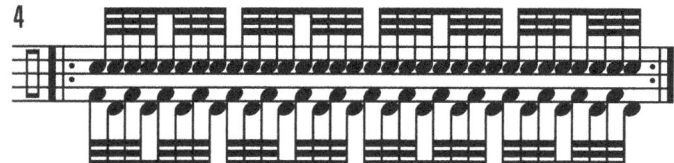

Playing grooves that incorporate fives or nines with the feet can be difficult. A good way to even them out is to play double-stroke rolls on top, as in Examples 5–8.

This concept will work with all duple- and triplet-based rolls. Our feet are more ambidextrous than our hands. We favor our strong hand in daily activities—we open doors, comb our hair, and write with our strong hand. But even if we always start with the same foot when we walk, the other one is right behind. Just remember to start slowly and be sure that you can mentally hear the rhythms before you play them. Then the feet are sure to follow.

Double Bass Time Line

The following time line covers some of the most important double bass drummers and the era in which they made their biggest contribution. Today's double bass players owe a great deal to these gentlemen.

The 1940s

Ray McKinley

In 1940 Ray McKinley, who at the time was playing with The Will Bradley Orchestra, added a second Slingerland 12x24 bass drum to his standard kit. While being one of the first to use two bass drums, McKinley abandoned the idea when he found that playing them in constant 8th notes was not very musically satisfying.

The 1950s

Louie Bellson

Louie Bellson secured a permanent role for two bass drums during his tenure with The Duke Ellington Orchestra. Playing either a pair of 24" or 26" Gretsch bass drums, Bellson made drum history with his riveting performance on the drum feature "Skin Deep."

The 1960s

Ginger Baker

Ginger Baker inspired a whole generation of drummers to play double bass. His innovative work with the band Cream pushed forward the rhythmic possibilities of double bass drumming. His lengthy solo on the group's extended jam "Toad" is a classic.

Keith Moon

Although not a dominant double bass drummer, Keith Moon was one of the early pioneers of rock 'n' roll double bass drumming. His massive Premier setups got drummers thinking about adding that second bass drum—and many more toms, too!

Carmine Appice

Carmine Appice brought a funkier, more R&B feel to double bass drumming. Excellent hand/foot coordination can be heard on "The Break Song" from Vanilla Fudge's album *Near The Beginning*.

Ed Shaughnessy

Ed Shaughnessy's double bass drumming could be seen and heard every weeknight on The Tonight Show with Johnny Carson. Along with Louie Bellson, Shaughnessy helped popularize double bass drumming in big band music.

Cozy Powell

Cozy Powell's powerful use of double bass and his innovative "quads" (right hand left hand, right foot, left foot combinations) can be heard on his many solo records and on albums by Jeff Beck and Rainbow.

The 1970s

Tommy Aldridge
Tommy Aldridge's innovative use of "threes" (three quick notes played on two bass drums within hand patterns), as well as a focused double bass approach, can be heard on albums by Black Oak Arkansas, Pat Travers, and Whitesnake.

Dom Famularo
International clinician and educator. Drumming's global ambassador. Known for his killer fast feet.

Billy Cobham
Billy Cobham introduced double bass drumming to the world of fusion music. Cobham's formidable playing can be heard on The Mahavishnu Orchestra's Birds Of Fire and on many of his solo albums of that period, including *Spectrum*, *Total Eclipse*, *A Funky Thide Of Sings*, and *Magic*.

Narada Michael Walden
Like Billy Cobham, Narada Michael Walden helped introduce and expand on the use of double bass in fusion. Examples of his groove and power can be heard on The Mahavishnu Orchestra's album *Visions Of The Emerald Beyond* and Jeff Beck's *Wired*.

Encyclopedia Of Double Bass Drumming | 105

Terry Bozzio

Terry Bozzio's dynamic rhythmic complexity and simply amazing use of double bass drum flams and ostinatos can be heard on his work with Frank Zappa, The Brecker Brothers, and Missing Persons.

Neil Peart

Neil Peart's impressive double bass work with progressive rock band Rush inspired legions of drummers to add a second kick drum to their setups. Peart "sprinkled" double bass throughout the band's music, and he used them liberally within his expansive solos.

Rod Morgenstein

Always a favorite in *Modern Drummer* polls, Rod creatively and tastefully integrated double bass drumming in his work with The Dixie Dregs, and later with The Steve Morse Band and Winger.

The 1980s

Simon Phillips

Simon Phillips' killing shuffle on Jeff Beck's "Space Boogie" set the standard for double bass shuffles. Simon is considered to be one of the most important double bass drummers, and his amazing work with artists like Pete Townshend, Jack Bruce, and Stanley Clarke proves it.

106 | Encyclopedia Of Double Bass Drumming

Steve Smith

Steve Smith's use of double bass drums can be heard in a variety of musical situations, from the hit-oriented songs of Journey to his own fusion group, Vital Information. While being an all-around great player, Steve's also recognized as an excellent double bass drum soloist.

Alex Van Halen

Although the band Van Halen began in the late '70s, Alex's double bass drumming is showcased on the song "Hot For Teacher" from the band's *1984* album.

Joe Franco

Joe Franco is the author of the excellent method book *Double Bass Drumming*. This breakthrough work was first published in 1984.

Lars Ulrich

Lars Ulrich's double bass drumming established a new standard in heavy metal drumming. Lars' speed and power can be heard on all of Metallica's albums from this era.

Gregg Bissonette

Bissonette came to the attention of the drumming community through his solid work with Maynard Ferguson, but his fabulous skill on two bass drums was really showcased when he was with David Lee Roth. Gregg is recognized today as one of the most musical double bass drummers.

Dave Lombardo

Considered one of the leading lights of the speed metal genre, Lombardo's double bass work with Slayer was impressive. The devastating speed and aggression Dave unleashed on his massive kit won him many fans.

Dennis Chambers

Chambers' creative use of the double pedal can be heard on recordings by John Scofield and many others. Excellent foot technique adds power and excitement to one of today's most complete and explosive drummers.

The 1990s

Vinnie Paul

Vinnie Paul's work with Pantera is impressive for the sheer speed he generates. Vinnie's feet are blazing.

Tim "Herb" Alexander

During his tenure with the "twisted" rock trio Primus, Tim "Herb" Alexander created some of the most original sounding double bass patterns ever recorded.

Danny Carey

Danny Carey is the force behind Tool. His uncompromising force and fluid feel while playing polyrhythms and odd meters has established him as one of the best drummers of his generation.

Nick Menza

Nick Menza is the former drummer for the thrash metal band Megadeth. He recorded on four of Megadeth's albums.

Chris Adler

Chris Adler is the founder of the heavy metal band Lamb of God. He is recognized for his open-handed technique, his use of the heel-toe technique, and his unusual approach to the drum kit as a left-handed player on a right-handed kit.

Mike Mangini

Mike Mangini joined Dream Theater after a very competitive auditioning process. Between 2002 and 2005, he set five World's Fastest Drummer records.

Thomas Lang

Thomas Lang is the founding member of the progressive/avant garde metal band stOrk. This Austrian drummer is celebrated for his notable hand and feet technique.

Mike Portnoy

Dream Theater's progressive rock approach receives an extra kick thanks to the powerful double bass work of Mike Portnoy. Mike has an uncanny ability to play a lot of double bass within the band's material and yet make it work on a musical level.

Carter Beauford

The Dave Matthews Band's Carter Beauford has increased the "visibility" of double-pedal technique. His use of double pedal within this popular band's music has excited a whole new generation of drummers.

Virgil Donati

Virgil Donati has set a new standard for double bass drum technique. His extraordinary use of double strokes and polyrhythmic patterns in his feet is revolutionary.

Marco Minnemann

German drummer Marco Minnemann is best known for developing a very advanced drum technique called "Extreme Interdependence". He is the author of several instructional books describing this concept.

Jason Bittner

Jason Bittner is recognized for his ability to play complex patterns at high speeds. He can be heard on the recordings of Overkill and Shadows Fall.

George Kollias

George Kolllias is a Greek heavy metal drummer and music teacher best known for his work with the technical death metal band Nile. He teaches drums at the Modern Music School in Athens, Greece.

Encyclopedia Of Double Bass Drumming

Thomas Haake

Tomas Haake is the Swedish drummer of the extreme metal band Meshuggah. He is known for his polyrhythmic skills and technical ability. The song "Bleed" is a masterpiece in terms of footwork.

Tim Waterson

Tim Waterson held the world record for the fastest number of double strokes on a bass drum, with a record of 1,407 in one minute (January 22, 2002). The Canadian drummer uses the heel-toe technique and also invented the pump technique for fast single strokes. Tim originally introduced Bobby to the heel/toe method.

John Micelli

John is one of the first drummers to use Turnarounds, which are very powerful patterns. Meat Loaf, Blue Oyster Cult, Rainbow, and Brian May are a few of John's credits.

Double Bass Discography

The following is a brief list of some of the best double bass performances captured on record. We highly recommend that you check out as many of these as possible.

Chris Adler
with Lamb of God: *Sacrament, Ashes of the Wake*

Tommy Aldridge
with Black Oak Arkansas: *If An Angel Came To See You, Would You Make Her Feel At Home, Raunch & Roll Live, High On The Hog*
with Pat Travers: *Go For What You Know*
with Whitesnake: *Slip Of The Tongue*

Tim "Herb" Alexander
with Primus: *Sailing The Seas Of Cheese, Pork Soda*

Carmine Appice
with Vanilla Fudge: *Near The Beginning, Vanilla Fudge*
with Jeff Beck: *Beck, Bogert & Appice*
with Blue Murder: *Blue Murder*

Ginger Baker
with Cream: *Wheels Of Fire, Best Of Cream*
with Blind Faith: *Blind Faith*

Carter Beauford
with The Dave Matthews Band: *Remember Two Things, Crash*

Louie Bellson
with Duke Ellington: *Ellington, Uptown*

Gregg Bissonette
with David Lee Roth: *A Little Ain't Enough, Eat 'Em And Smile, Skyscraper.*
with Frank Gambale: *Thunder From Down Under*

Terry Bozzio
with Frank Zappa: *Live in New York, Sheik Yerbouti, You Can't Do That On Stage, Vols. I-IV*
with The Brecker Brothers: *Heavy Metal BeBop*
with Missing Persons: *The Best Of*

Danny Carey
With Tool: *Ænima, Lateralus*

Dennis Chambers
with John Scofield: *Pick Hits Live*

Billy Cobham
with the Mahavishnu Orchestra: *Birds of Fire*
as a leader: *Spectrum, Total Eclipse, A Funky Thide of Sings, Magic*

Vinnie Colaiuta
with Warren Cuccurullo: *Th@n.ks 2:/Fr@nk*
as a leader: *Vinnie Colaiuta*

Joe Franco
with Widowmaker- *Blood & Bullets* "Emaheevul"
with Vinnie Moore- *Time Odyssey* "Race with Destiny"

Tomas Haake
with Meshuggah: *obZen, Koloss*

Joey Jordison
with Slipknot: *Slipknot, Iowa*

Dave Lombardo
with Slayer: *Reign In Blood, South Of Heaven, Seasons In The Abyss*

Mike Mangini
with Dream Theater: A *Dramatic Turn of Events, The Astonishing*

Ray McKinley
with Will Bradley: *The Best Of The Big Band*

Rod Morgenstein
with The Dixie Dregs: *What If, Night Of The Living Dregs*
with Winger: *Winger, In The Heart Of The Young*

Vinnie Paul
with Pantera: *Vulgar Display Of Power, Far Beyond Driven*

Mike Portnoy
with Dream Theater: *When Dream And Day Unite, Images And Words, Awake, Falling Into Infinity*
with Liquid Tension Experiment: *Liquid Tension Experiment, Liquid Tension Experiment 2*

Neil Peart
with Rush: *All The Worlds A Stage, Exit... Stage Left*

Simon Phillips
with Jeff Beck: *There & Back*
with Pete Townshend: *Empty Glass*
with Stanley Clarke: *Rocks, Pebbles & Sand*

Cozy Powell
with Jeff Beck: Jeff Beck Group, *Rough & Ready*
with Rainbow: *Rising, On Stage*

Ed Shaughnessy
with Doc Severinsen: *Swingin' The Blues*

Steve Smith
with Journey: *Captured, Escape*
with Tony MacAlpine: *Edge Of Insanity*
as a leader (Vital Information): *Vitalive!*

Lars Ulrich
with Metallica: Kill 'Em All, *Ride The Lightning, Master Of Puppets, ...And Justice For All*

Alex Van Halen
with Van Halen: *Van Halen, Van Halen II, 1984*

Narada Michael Walden
with The Mahavishnu Orchestra: *Visions Of The Emerald Beyond*
with Jeff Beck: *Wired*

BEST SELLING DRUM TITLES WORLDWIDE

  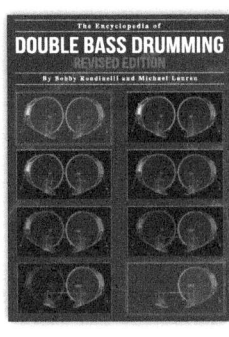   

 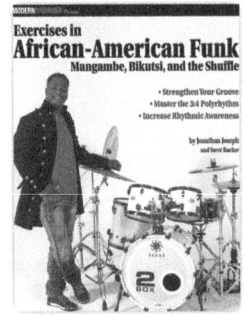  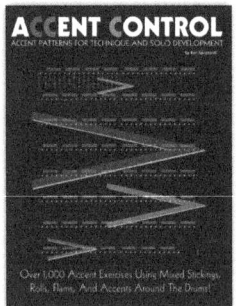  
 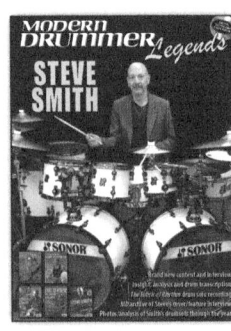    

Available in print and digital format at **moderndrummer.com** or from your favorite music retailer